"*No Quick Fix* is superb! Readers may not know Keswick theology by name, but many Christians in Britain and North America have been influenced by its teachings regardless. If you want to explore a truly biblical understanding of progressive sanctification while avoiding the pitfalls of some popular well-intended but misguided teachings, you'll benefit greatly from this book. I enthusiastically recommend Naselli's winsome, insightful, and instructive treatment and pray many will grow in their Christian lives as a result of giving careful attention to this book."

—BRUCE A. WARE, T. Rupert and Lucille Coleman Professor of Christian Theology, chairman of the Department of Christian Theology, The Southern Baptist Theological Seminary

"For years popular Christian teachers have been enticing us with the 'secret key' to the victorious, higher, deeper, more abundant Christian life. We've been told just to 'let go and let God.' If you've heard that teaching, you'll want to read this clear and accessible book. You'll learn not only where this well-intentioned teaching goes wrong, but you will discover afresh the well-worn old paths of biblical faithfulness and holiness. Andy Naselli is a careful scholar and a compassionate guide who longs to help and serve the church of Jesus Christ. I predict you will not be disappointed."

—JUSTIN TAYLOR, executive vice president of book publishing and book publisher, Crossway

"I am so pleased to see this work in print. For years I have required my doctoral students to read the original academic version of this incredibly helpful work. Now it's finally available to everyone in a more accessible format. It is so clear, concise, well-organized, and understandable that anyone interested in an evaluation of the 'higher life' movement—educators, students, pastors, or laymen— can profit from Andy's research. No one who wants to know more about this influential movement can afford to be without this valuable resource."

—DONALD S. WHITNEY, professor of biblical spirituality and associate dean of the School of Theology, The Southern Baptist Theological Seminary

"Some books on the Christian life are practical ... but shallow. Others are profound ... but so dense they put you to sleep. This book is both 'practical' and 'gripping.' It will draw in any reader who has wrestled with the how-to of spiritual growth. Read this for rich insights, challenge, and encouragement regarding yourself and God's wondrous movements on your behalf to transform your life and soul."

—ROBERT W. YARBROUGH, professor of New Testament, Covenant Theological Seminary

"Every Christian struggles with sin. How to deal with and overcome it serves as the central question for higher life teachers. But do they have the right answer? Andy Naselli's comprehensive analysis of higher life theology provides us with sufficient evidence that they do not. While the higher life quick fix to the sin problem would be nice, Andy gives us ten reasons why this theology is so harmful. And the appendix provides an abundance of helpful resources to encourage believers in their Christian walk. If frustration, confusion, and irritation are words that describe your battle with sin, especially if you've been seeking an easy way to victory, then you need to read this book."

—JON PRATT, vice president of academics and professor
of New Testament, Central Baptist Theological Seminary;
elder, Eden Baptist Church (Burnsville, MN)

"When I was in high school, I ordered a book called *They Found the Secret*, which described the second blessing experience of twenty godly people. I wanted the kind of victory over sin and communion with Christ the book described, but the breakthrough experiences they described remained elusive. I wondered if I was somehow a 'less-than' Christian. *No Quick Fix* finally made sense of what I read in that book as well as much of the other teaching I received in my early years that came out of camps heavily influenced by higher life theology. By explaining the teaching and its fallacies, as well as giving the history and personalities behind it, this book not only fascinated me; it also equipped me to recognize this faulty teaching when I see it and to replace it with a more solidly biblical perspective."

—NANCY GUTHRIE, Bible teacher and author

"In this condensed and repackaged version of his earlier work on Keswick theology (*Let Go and Let God?*) Andy Naselli provides a spiritual feast for those of us who are serious about following Christ and living the Christian life. His main focus is the doctrine of sanctification, but this is not a dry academic treatment of that theological topic. His presentation is engaging, and throughout the book he provides practical instruction for the everyday questions and struggles of the Christian life. He also addresses a host of related themes that are extremely important for Christians, including perfectionism, free will, Spirit-filling, abiding in Christ, and false assurance. If you are serious about living the Christian life and ministering to others who are struggling in their Christian experience, then *No Quick Fix* is a book you need to read."

—W. EDWARD GLENNY, professor of New Testament Studies
and Greek, University of Northwestern (St. Paul, MN)

"*No Quick Fix* is more than a catchy title—it captures a profound biblical truth with significant ramifications for personal spiritual growth, our view of discipleship, and the overall health of local congregations. Much of contemporary Christianity, sadly, has been shaped by a culture wired for immediate gratification and a perpetual parade of spiritual quick fixes offering some combination of 'secrets' and 'steps' that will guarantee immediate spiritual victory. Andy Naselli has done a great service to the church in tracing the roots of this quick-fix theology and graciously, yet clearly, exposing its errors. Andy offers an evenhanded critique that does a wonderful job of putting together a thorough explanation of the various stands and unifying features of Keswick teaching. He has listened carefully to Keswick's arguments before answering them with equal care. Bad theology hinders spiritual growth and hurts discipleship. *No Quick Fix* shines the light of Scripture on some bad ideas that have frustrated believers for decades. Releasing believers from false burdens and expectations sets them free to pursue Christlikeness. Real growth and real discipleship will be strengthened by this book. I highly recommend it!"

—DAVID M. DORAN, senior pastor, Inter-City Baptist Church
(Allen Park, MI); president and chairman of the Practical
Theology Department, Detroit Baptist Theological Seminary

"*No Quick Fix* offers an introduction to the falsities of higher life theology that is important for those in both the pulpit and the pew to read. Accessible and filled with simplifying charts, lists, and graphics, Naselli's retooled dissertation provides a solid, biblical understanding of sanctification. It exalts the grace of God in Christ, counters contemporary expressions of Pelagianism, and exposes the weaknesses of a two-tiered 'mature' vs. 'carnal' Christianity. Believers who are intentional in disciple-making especially will find this book rewarding."

—ERIC C. REDMOND, assistant professor of Bible, Moody Bible Institute

"Throughout the world people are desperately searching for the higher life, the deeper life, and their best life now. The nineteenth-century theology associated with the Keswick movement brings many dangers, and it is alive and well in the twenty-first century and running rampant in many churches. This insightful and scholarly work by Dr. Andrew David Naselli is well suited for professors and pastors as well as for the concerned layperson. Naselli provides a gracious and thorough assessment of various aberrant views of sanctification while offering reasoned, biblical exegetical conclusions on this most vital doctrine of the faith once delivered to the saints."

—BURK PARSONS, co-pastor of Saint Andrew's Chapel
(Sanford, FL); editor of *Tabletalk* magazine

NO QUICK FIX

Where Higher Life Theology Came From,
What It Is, and Why It's Harmful

Andrew David Naselli

LEXHAM PRESS

No Quick Fix: Where Higher Life Theology Came From, What It Is, and Why It's Harmful

Copyright 2017 Andrew David Naselli

Lexham Press, 1313 Commercial St., Bellingham, WA 98225
LexhamPress.com

Print ISBN 9781683590460
Digital ISBN 9781577997283

Lexham Editorial Team: Elliot Ritzema, Jennifer Edwards
Cover Design: Bryan Hintz
Typesetting: ProjectLuz.com

Contents

List of Figures

To Jenni,
My second blessing

Introduction

It is not much of a recommendation when all you can say is that this teaching may help you if you do not take its details too seriously. It is utterly damning to have to say, as in this case I think we must, that if you do take its details seriously, it will tend not to help you but to destroy you.[1]

That's what the influential theologian J. I. Packer wrote about higher life theology. It has harmed many people—including me.

I TRIED TO "LET GO AND LET GOD"

I'm not sure when God first enabled me to turn from my sins and trust Jesus. I probably became a Christian when I was eight or twelve years old. In my teen years, I deeply desired to be holy. I wanted to serve God with my heart and soul and mind and strength. I didn't want to waste my life.

When I shared my Christian "testimony" in my high school and early college years, I would say something like this: "God *saved* me from my sins when I was eight years old, and I *surrendered* to Christ when I was thirteen." By "saved," I meant Jesus became my Savior, and I became a Christian. By "surrendered," I meant I dedicated myself to Jesus—I finally gave full control of my life to Jesus as my Master and yielded to do whatever he wanted me to do.

Most of the Christians I knew—especially preachers—used those categories, so I did, too. Young people in my youth groups or at summer camp commonly told their stories the same way: "I accepted Christ as my *Savior* when I was eight years old, and I accepted Christ as my *Lord* when I was thirteen." That was the standard God-talk lingo.

---

1. J. I. Packer, *Keep in Step with the Spirit: Finding Fullness in Our Walk with God*, 2nd ed. (Grand Rapids: Baker Books, 2005), 130.

There were always two steps: first you get *saved*; then you get *serious*. Too many of us Christians were saved but not serious. We were living a lower life rather than a higher life, a shallow life rather than a deeper life, a defeated life rather than a victorious life, a fruitless life rather than a more abundant life. We were "carnal," not "spiritual." We experienced the first blessing but still needed the second blessing. Jesus was our Savior, but he still wasn't our Master. So preachers urged us to make Jesus our Master. How? Through surrender and faith: "Let go and let God."

The small Bible college I attended as an undergraduate was a ministry of my church, and preachers in my college and church took this carnal-spiritual dichotomy to another level. It became their primary focus and distinctive passion. Whether the text was from Exodus, Jeremiah, Matthew, or Revelation, nearly every sermon had the same application to Christians: Be Spirit-filled. That's *the* key.

At first, I genuinely tried to go along with the program, but it just didn't work for me. During my freshman and sophomore years of college, I became frustrated, then disillusioned, and then suspicious. I became frustrated because I still struggled with sin. I became disillusioned because higher life theology seemed too good to be true. And I became suspicious because this teaching didn't seem to fit with what I was reading in the Bible.

I appealed to one of my former pastors for guidance, and he guided me safely through this storm. He recommended books, articles, sermons, and syllabi from his seminary, and I devoured them. By the time I was a senior in college, my school's president and vice president nearly expelled me for not embracing their two-tiered view of Christian living.

EVALUATING HIGHER LIFE THEOLOGY

I entered graduate school with this issue on my front burner. I wanted to go deeper, so I wrote several research papers related to the topic as I completed an MA in Bible and then worked on a PhD in theology. I met more and more people who were victims of higher life theology, and I became aware of even more people who continued to propagate it.

So when it came time to choose a dissertation topic, I decided to evaluate higher life theology. I wrote a dissertation that surveys the history and theology of that two-tiered view of progressive sanctification and then analyzes it.[2] Then I lightly revised that dissertation as a book for Lexham Press: *Let Go and Let God? A Survey and Analysis of Keswick Theology*.[3]

This book is a miniature version of my more detailed and academic work *Let Go and Let God?* I have stripped out most of the academic jargon and repackaged it to make it more inviting for thoughtful lay people.[4] For example, I usually use the term *higher life theology* instead of *Keswick theology* since higher life theology is a more intuitive label. I also want to be careful to distinguish higher life theology from the Keswick Convention today.[5] (By the way, *Keswick* is pronounced KEH-zick. The *w* is silent.)

I have become more and more convinced that the "let go and let God" approach to Christian living is a quick fix. A *quick fix*, according to the *Oxford English Dictionary*, is "a quick and easy remedy or solution"—or negatively, "an expedient but temporary solution which fails to address underlying problems." That's what I think higher life theology is—an easy but temporary remedy or solution that fails to address underlying problems. And that's why the title of this book is *No Quick Fix*.

---

2. Andrew David Naselli, "Keswick Theology: A Historical and Theological Survey and Analysis of the Doctrine of Sanctification in the Early Keswick Movement, 1875–1920" (PhD diss., Bob Jones University, 2006). I later condensed the dissertation to about twenty percent of its original size for a journal article: Andrew David Naselli, "Keswick Theology: A Survey and Analysis of the Doctrine of Sanctification in the Early Keswick Movement," *Detroit Baptist Seminary Journal* 13 (2008): 17–67.
3. Andrew David Naselli, *Let Go and Let God? A Survey and Analysis of Keswick Theology* (Bellingham, WA: Lexham Press, 2010). It's available exclusively from Logos Bible Software (in electronic format, not in print format).
4. I do not exhaustively (and exhaustingly) footnote what I assert in this book, so researchers looking for primary and secondary sources should consult *Let Go and Let God?* Chapter 1 surveys previous works (pp. 49–72); the rest of the book interacts extensively with primary and secondary sources (mainly pp. 76–295); and a relatively comprehensive bibliography concludes the book (pp. 328–459).
5. Keswick is a small town in northwest England, and since 1875, it has hosted a weeklong meeting in July for the Keswick Convention. From 1875 to about 1920, those meetings featured higher life theology. Beginning in the 1920s, the Keswick Convention's view of sanctification began to shift from the view that the leaders of the early Keswick Convention promoted from 1875 to 1920. William Graham Scroggie (1877–1958) led that transformation to a view of progressive sanctification closer to the Reformed view. More recently its speakers have included people like Don Carson, Tim Chester, and Sinclair Ferguson, whose views on the Christian life differ significantly from the early Keswick movement.

WHY IS HIGHER LIFE THEOLOGY SO POPULAR?

My story is not unique. Hundreds of Christians have shared their stories with me about how higher life theology has harmed them. I have tried to do my part to drive a nail in the coffin of higher life theology, but higher life theology is by no means dead. So if higher life theology is so harmful, why is it so popular?

It is pervasive because countless people have propagated it in so many ways, especially in sermons and devotional writings. It is appealing because Christians struggle with sin and want to be victorious in that struggle—now. Higher life theology offers a quick fix to this struggle, and its shortcut to instant victory appeals to people who genuinely desire to be holy.

WHO SHOULD READ THIS BOOK?

This book is for you if you have a form of higher life theology in your background. You may embrace higher life theology enthusiastically; you may embrace it unknowingly; you may know there's something not right about it but can't clearly explain why; or you may reject it and would like to analyze it more penetratingly.

This book is also for you if you *don't* have a form of higher life theology in your background. Higher life theology is so widespread that you will be able to serve your brothers and sisters in Christ better if you understand what it is and why it's dangerous.

A silver lining of theological controversy is that it can help you refine how you understand what the Bible teaches. In this case, analyzing higher life theology will help you better understand the Christian life.

HOW THIS BOOK EVALUATES HIGHER LIFE THEOLOGY

This book has two parts. Part 1 tells the story of higher life theology (chap. 1) and explains what it is (chap. 2). Part 2 evaluates whether higher life theology agrees with the Bible (chaps. 3-4).

My goal is not to make you an arrogant know-it-all who pugnaciously goes on higher life theology witch hunts. My goal is to edify you by warning and equipping you. I'll consider this book a success if it helps you understand higher life theology better so that you follow a more biblical way in your Christian walk (see the appendix). There is no quick fix.

Where Higher Life Theology Came From and What It Is

Before we can responsibly evaluate higher life theology (part 2), we must understand it. We must listen before we critique. So part 1 tells the story of where higher life theology came from (chap. 1) and explains what exactly it is (chap. 2).

CHAPTER 1

What Is the Story of
Higher Life Theology?

When I first heard people preach and teach higher life theology, I didn't know anything about its story. My pastors and other teachers claimed the Bible teaches higher life theology, so I initially assumed that they were right and that Christians have always embraced it. Learning its history was a liberating step for me. I realized that this view is novel—that it is relatively new in the history of Christianity. It is also just one of several competing views about Christian living.

There are at least five major views that evangelicals hold on the Christian life.[1] At the risk of oversimplifying them, five figures presented throughout this book attempt to graphically depict those views of Christian living, which theologians call views of sanctification (see figs. 1.2, 1.3, 1.5, 2.4, and 3.8).[2]

---

1. By *evangelicals*, I mean people who affirm the *evangel*—the gospel. See D. A. Carson, "The Biblical Gospel," in *For Such a Time as This: Perspectives on Evangelicalism, Past, Present and Future*, ed. Steve Brady and Harold Rowdon (London: Evangelical Alliance, 1996), 75-85; Carson, "What Is the Gospel?—Revisited," in *For the Fame of God's Name: Essays in Honor of John Piper*, ed. Sam Storms and Justin Taylor (Wheaton, IL: Crossway, 2010), 147-70. I recognize that there is a broad spectrum of people who identify as evangelicals. See Andrew David Naselli and Collin Hansen, eds., *Four Views on the Spectrum of Evangelicalism*, Counterpoints (Grand Rapids: Zondervan, 2011).

2. Adapted from Charles C. Ryrie, *Balancing the Christian Life*, 2nd ed. (Chicago: Moody, 1994), 191-200; H. Wayne House, *Charts of Christian Theology and Doctrine* (Grand Rapids: Zondervan, 1992), 111-13.

This chapter tells the story of higher life theology by answering three main questions:

1. Where did higher life theology come from?
2. Who initially popularized higher life theology?
3. What are some influential variations on higher life theology?

The story begins with John Wesley.

1. WHERE DID HIGHER LIFE THEOLOGY COME FROM?

Figure 1.1 illustrates where higher life theology came from:

Fig. 1.1. Where Did Higher Life Theology Come From?

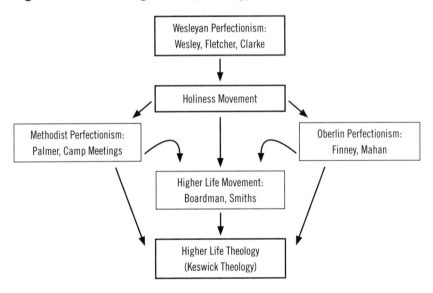

Higher life theology has two main influences: Wesleyan perfectionism and the holiness movement.

WESLEYAN PERFECTIONISM: PERFECT LOVE TOWARD GOD AND HUMANS

The Wesleyan view of progressive sanctification has a lot in common with higher life theology. John Wesley (1703-1791) is the father of views that chronologically separate the time a person becomes a Christian from the time sanctification begins.

Wesley taught "Christian perfection," which he qualifies does *not* refer to absolute sinless perfection.[3] *Christian* perfection is a type of perfection that only Christians can experience—as opposed to Adamic perfection, angelic perfection, or God's unique, absolute perfection. The way Wesley qualifies Christian perfection hinges on how he narrowly defines sin as "a voluntary transgression of a known law." He limits "sin" to only *intentional* sinful acts. He admits that "the best of men" commit "involuntary transgressions," for which they need Christ's atonement, but he can still call such people perfect or sinless. When one defines sin that way, Wesley does not object to the term "sinless perfection," but he refrains from using that term because it is misleading.[4]

The essence of Wesley's Christian perfection is perfectly loving God with your whole being and, consequently, perfectly loving fellow humans. Christian perfection occurs at a point in time after you are already a Christian. Wesley labels this second work of grace as not only Christian perfection but salvation from all sin, entire sanctification, perfect love, holiness, purity of intention, full salvation, second blessing, second rest, and dedicating all your life to God (see fig. 1.2).[5]

---

3. John Wesley, "A Plain Account of Christian Perfection, as Believed and Taught by the Reverend Mr. John Wesley, from the Year 1725, to the Year 1777," in *The Works of John Wesley*, 3rd ed., 14 vols. (London: Wesleyan Methodist Book Room, 1872), 11:375, 442.

4. Ibid., 11:396, 418, 442.

5. This is the first of five figures illustrating major views that evangelicals hold on the Christian life. I explain figures 1.2, 1.3, and 1.5 in this chapter, focus on figure 2.4 in chapter 2, and defend figure 3.8 in chapter 3. The cross in each figure represents the point in time when a person first repents of their sin and believes in Jesus. The dotted arrows in the first three figures show that a person may repeatedly lose and recover the state that results from the crisis.

Fig. 1.2. The Wesleyan View of Sanctification

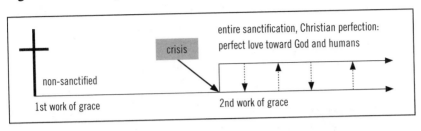

Two of Wesley's followers significantly developed his doctrine of Christian perfection. John Fletcher (1729–1785) used "Pentecostal" language to describe how Christian perfection begins the instant a believer experiences the outpouring of the Spirit, is baptized with the Spirit, is filled with the Spirit, or receives the Holy Spirit as the promise from the Father. Adam Clarke (1762–1832) used Fletcher's "Pentecostal" language to emphasize the crisis of Christian perfection more than both Wesley and Fletcher.

THE HOLINESS MOVEMENT: MODIFIED WESLEYAN PERFECTIONISM

When Wesleyan perfectionism blended with American revivalism, the holiness movement emerged. The holiness movement began in the late 1830s and modified the views of Wesley, Fletcher, and Clarke. Two significant parts of the holiness movement were Methodist perfectionism and Oberlin perfectionism.

Methodist perfectionism emphasized the crisis of Christian perfection more emphatically than Wesleyan perfectionism. The person most responsible for that was Phoebe Palmer (1807–1874). Her "altar theology" promised "a shorter way" to holiness.

The term *altar theology* comes from the first step of Palmer's popular three-step teaching: You must entirely consecrate yourself or totally surrender by offering yourself and all you have on the altar (Rom 12:1–2). Christ is the altar (Exod 29:37; Heb 13:10), and the altar sanctifies the offering (Matt 23:19). When you entirely consecrate yourself, you are instantly and entirely sanctified.

Palmer used "Pentecostal" language to emphasize the crisis of Christian perfection, which she argued results in power for serving God. Her views became popular through her writings and through holiness camp meetings that began in New Jersey in 1867. During these holiness camp meetings, revivalists pressed people to choose to experience the crisis of entire sanctification.

Oberlin perfectionism is similar to Wesleyan perfectionism, but it distinctively views sanctification as entirely consecrating a person's autonomous free will to obey the moral law. Its two main proponents were Charles Finney (1792–1875) and Asa Mahan (1799–1889).[6] They taught that Christian perfection begins with a crisis of Spirit-baptism that Christians should experience at a point in time after they first become Christians.

Finney embraced Pelagianism, which denies that humans are totally depraved and views them as able to obey any of God's commands without God's help. The preacher's task is to persuade their autonomous free will to obey. Under the heading "Entire Sanctification Is Attainable in This Life," Finney asserts, "It is self-evident that entire obedience to God's law is possible on the ground of natural ability."[7]

Mahan names two doctrines as the theme of his life: Christian perfection and the baptism of the Holy Spirit.[8] He emphasized that unbelievers benefit from justification at conversion and that believers benefit from sanctification sometime after conversion when they are Spirit-baptized.

Mahan had both theological affinities and personal connections with both Methodist perfectionism and higher life theology. He endorsed Phoebe Palmer's *The Way of Holiness*, and the Palmers published his *The Baptism of the Holy Ghost* (1870). After he moved to England in 1872, he helped lead the higher life movement, which immediately preceded the first Keswick Convention in 1875.

2. WHO INITIALLY POPULARIZED HIGHER LIFE THEOLOGY?

Higher life theology includes the higher life movement (1858–1875) and culminated in the early Keswick movement (1875–1920). Both movements represented a number of different Christian denominations rather than

---

6. The term *Oberlin perfectionism* comes from Oberlin College. Mahan was Oberlin's first president (1835–1850), and Finney was its second president (1851–1866) and first theology professor (1835–1866).

7. Charles G. Finney, *Lectures on Systematic Theology* (Oberlin: Fitch, 1847), 204.

8. Asa Mahan, *Autobiography, Intellectual, Moral, and Spiritual* (London: Woolmer, 1882), 320–21.

just one. Higher life theology modified Wesleyan, Methodist, and Oberlin perfectionism in a way that appealed more broadly to non-Methodists: it referred to the higher Christian life instead of Christian perfection.

THE HIGHER LIFE MOVEMENT

The higher life movement began in 1858 when William Boardman's popular book *The Higher Christian Life* released, and it dissolved in 1875 when its leaders removed Robert Pearsall Smith from public ministry.

William E. Boardman (1810–1886). Phoebe Palmer, Charles Finney, and Asa Mahan strongly influenced how Boardman understood the Christian life. Boardman professed that God justified him when he was eighteen and sanctified him when he was thirty-two. The essence of the higher Christian life is separating justification from sanctification. Boardman equated Spirit-baptism with the "second conversion," and his best-known book, *The Higher Christian Life*, sold over 100,000 copies in less than thirty years. He began and led the higher life movement for over a decade until a husband-wife team—Robert and Hannah Smith—overshadowed him in the early 1870s.

Robert Pearsall Smith (1827–1898) and Hannah Whitall Smith (1832–1911). Robert and Hannah Smith zealously spread their crisis experiences with others through personal conversations, public speaking, and most enduringly through Hannah's writing. The message of her most influential book, *The Christian's Secret of a Happy Life*, is essentially two steps:

1. "entire surrender" or "entire abandonment" (i.e., "let go")
2. "absolute faith" (i.e., "let God")

As with Boardman, foundational to her message is separating justification (i.e., God's declaring a believing sinner righteous) and sanctification (i.e., Christian growth in holiness), which explains why she would appeal to "carnal" Christians to surrender to the Lord, who "is able to save you fully, now, in this life, from the power and dominion of sin."[9] Only *some* believers experience this crisis (which she identifies with Spirit-baptism). She explains,

---

9. Hannah Whitall Smith, *The Christian's Secret of a Happy Life*, 2nd ed. (Boston: Christian Witness, 1885), 22.

> This new life I had entered upon has been called by several different names. The Methodists called it "The Second Blessing," or "The Blessing of Sanctification;" the Presbyterians called it "The Higher Life," or "The Life of Faith;" the Friends called it "The Life hid with Christ in God." But by whatever name it may be called, the truth at the bottom of each name is the same, and can be expressed in four little words, "Not I, but Christ."[10]

Although *The Christian's Secret of a Happy Life* endures as a devotional "classic," Robert and Hannah Smith did not have "happy" lives. The Smith family experienced a series of sad events: (1) At the height of his success as a higher life revivalist, Robert fell doctrinally and morally. (2) Robert and Hannah's deteriorating marriage declined even further. Hannah's intense feminism and independence, Robert's manic-depressive nature, and Robert's persistence in unrepentant adultery all contributed to a very unhappy marriage. (3) Robert apostatized and became an agnostic. (4) Hannah apostatized. She lost interest in the higher life, rejoined the Quakers in 1886, and embraced universalism and religious pluralism.[11]

While the Smiths were popular writers on their own, what "institutionalized the message of the Smiths"[12] was the Keswick Convention.

THE EARLY KESWICK MOVEMENT

The higher life theology of Boardman and the Smiths captivated T. D. Harford-Battersby. Through a sermon that Evan Hopkins preached on John 4:46–50 at a meeting that Robert Pearsall Smith led in 1874, Harford-Battersby experienced his crisis on September 1, 1874. Hopkins

---

10. Hannah Whitall Smith, *The Unselfishness of God and How I Discovered It: A Spiritual Autobiography* (New York: Revell, 1903), 261.

11. Interesting aside: When I was first researching Hannah Whitall Smith, I was surprised to learn that my wife, Jennifer Joy (Becker) Naselli, is related to Hannah through both the Whitall line (Hannah's mother) and the Mickle line (Hannah's father). Jenni is Hannah's second cousin six generations removed. I don't hold it against her!

12. Mary Agnes Rittenhouse Maddox, "'Jesus Saves Me Now': Sanctification in the Writings of Hannah Whitall Smith" (PhD diss., Southern Baptist Theological Seminary, 2003), 109.

distinguished between the nobleman's "seeking faith" and "resting faith" in John 4:46-50, and Harford-Battersby pointed to this as the moment when his "seeking faith" became a "resting faith." Harford-Battersby and Robert Wilson decided to hold a similar meeting in their hometown of Keswick, a small town in northwest England. They asked Robert Pearsall Smith to chair their meeting, but Smith fell from ministry just a few days before the first Keswick Convention began in 1875.

Keswick has hosted the week-long Keswick Convention each July since 1875. Dozens of people preached and taught at the Keswick Convention in its first generation (1875-1920), and all of them experienced a crisis in which they entered "the rest of faith." What follows highlights sixteen of higher life theology's most noteworthy and influential proponents. The first eight were convention leaders.

1-2. *T. D. Harford-Battersby (1823-1883) and Robert Wilson (1824-1905): Keswick's Founders.* Harford-Battersby and Wilson cofounded the Keswick Convention in 1875. Harford-Battersby chaired the Keswick meetings from 1875 until he died in 1883, and Wilson, later Keswick's third chairman, handled logistical details.

3. *J. Elder Cumming (1830-1917): Keswick's Exemplar.* Cumming was a minister with a reputation for being irritable. When he first visited the Keswick Convention in 1882, on two separate occasions some ladies who knew him expressed that they were delightfully surprised to see him there, implying that he needed what Keswick had to offer. He experienced his crisis that week and returned to speak at Keswick for the next twenty-four consecutive years until 1906. The revivalist D. L. Moody knew Cumming before his crisis in 1882 and considered him the "most cantankerous Christian [he] had ever met." When Moody visited Cumming in 1891, he remarked in disbelief, "Whatever has happened to Cumming? I have never seen a man so altered, so full of the love of God." When Moody learned that Cumming had been to Keswick, he replied, "Then

I only wish all other Christians would go to Keswick too, and get their hearts filled with the love of God."[13]

4.   *Evan H. Hopkins (1837–1918): Keswick's Formative Theologian.* Hopkins experienced his higher life crisis of surrender and faith in 1873 when Robert Pearsall Smith and William Boardman were informally speaking on the higher Christian life throughout England. A few years later it was Hopkins who was preaching when Harford-Battersby entered the "rest of faith" and then founded the Keswick Convention. Hopkins did not attend the first Keswick Convention because, as a member of the council of eight who dismissed Smith after his fall, Hopkins was occupied with replacing Smith as the new editor of *The Christian's Pathway to Power* (which he changed to *The Life of Faith*). But he appeared as a leader at the Keswick Convention for the next forty consecutive years (1876–1915). He was perhaps the single most respected and influential early Keswick leader, and he was Keswick's most formative theologian.

5.   *H. W. Webb-Peploe (1837–1923): Keswick's Orator.* Webb-Peploe, an Anglican clergyman, experienced his higher life crisis in 1874, and he spoke at twenty-eight Keswick Conventions. He was a popular speaker and perhaps Keswick's finest orator.

6.   *H. C. G. Moule (1841–1920): Keswick's Scholar.* Moule is the most prestigious scholar associated with the early Keswick movement. He was the principal of Ridley Hall in Cambridge (1880–1899) and the Bishop of Durham (1901–1920), and he wrote popular commentaries on Romans, Galatians, Ephesians, Philippians, and Colossians. He initially viewed the Keswick movement unfavorably: in 1884 he negatively reviewed Evan Hopkins's *The Law of Liberty in the Spiritual Life.* But later that year he experienced his crisis of surrender and faith after listening to Evan Hopkins preach. Moule spoke at the Keswick Convention thirteen times between 1886 and 1919.

---

13. J. C. Pollock, *The Keswick Story: The Authorized History of the Keswick Convention* (Chicago: Moody, 1964), 60–61.

7. *F. B. Meyer (1847–1929): Keswick's International Ambassador.* Meyer experienced his first crisis in 1884 and a second in 1887, illustrating the three steps he proclaimed that people should experience: (1) conversion, (2) consecration, and (3) the anointing of the Spirit. He spoke at the Keswick Convention twenty-six times, and as one of the world's most popular preachers, he was the worldwide spokesman for higher life theology. He authored over seventy popular books and booklets, and he helped spread higher life theology to America through D. L. Moody's annual Northfield Conference in Massachusetts.

8. *Charles A. Fox (1836–1900): Keswick's Poet.* Frequent illnesses prevented Fox from speaking at the Keswick Convention until 1879, after which he spoke every year through 1899 (except 1897). After his first convention, he gave the closing address on the final evening of each convention he attended. He was Keswick's poet, and his best-known poem was "The Marred Face."

The next eight people were not as prominent and regular speakers at the Keswick Convention as the eight above, but they were highly influential in spreading higher life theology.

9. *Andrew Murray (1828–1917): Keswick's Foremost Devotional Author.* Murray popularized higher life theology in South Africa. He attended the Keswick Convention as a listener in 1882 and a speaker in 1895, when as a prolific author he was by far the most popular speaker. He authored over 250 devotional books.

10–11. *J. Hudson Taylor (1832–1905) and Amy Carmichael (1867–1951): Keswick's Foremost Missionaries.* The Keswick Convention began to focus on both consecration and missions beginning in 1886–1887. Taylor, founder of the China Inland Mission, estimated that Keswick produced two-thirds of his missionaries. He experienced the higher life on September 4, 1869, after he read this phrase in a letter from a fellow missionary: "Not by striving after faith, but by resting on the Faithful

WHAT IS THE STORY OF HIGHER LIFE THEOLOGY?

One."[14] Taylor visited Keswick in 1883 and 1887 and officially spoke in 1893. The first missionary whom the Keswick Convention supported was Amy Carmichael, the adopted daughter of Keswick's cofounder Robert Wilson. She served in Japan for one year and in India for fifty-six, and she wrote over thirty-five books.

12. *Frances Ridley Havergal (1836–1879): Keswick's Hymnist.* After experiencing her crisis on December 2, 1873, Havergal became known as "the consecration poet," and she "thus was able before her early death to write those hymnal lyrics indelibly identified with Keswick: *Like a river glorious is God's perfect peace* [1878] and *Take my Life and let it be* [1874]."[15]

13. *A. T. Pierson (1837–1911): Keswick's American Ambassador.* Pierson did not experience his higher life crisis that identified him with the Keswick movement until 1895. He spoke at eight Keswick Conventions from 1897 to 1909, and he promoted Keswick theology in his writing and preaching, spreading it at key conferences, such as Northfield in America.

14–16. *W. H. Griffith Thomas (1861–1924), Charles G. Trumbull (1872–1941), and Robert C. McQuilkin (1886–1952): Keswick's Leaders of the Victorious Life Movement.* The victorious life movement was the American version of the Keswick movement (although it was not officially connected with the Keswick Convention). It began in 1913 and promoted higher life theology for decades. Its three primary leaders were Griffith Thomas, Trumbull, and McQuilkin. Griffith Thomas experienced his crisis at age eighteen, and he spoke at the Keswick Convention four times (1906–1908, 1914). He was the featured speaker at the first victorious life conference in 1913. Trumbull experienced his crisis in 1910 and enthusiastically promoted higher life theology in America. McQuilkin experienced his crisis on August 15, 1911, when Trumbull counseled him in a conference cen-

---

14. Howard Taylor and Geraldine Taylor, *Hudson Taylor and the China Inland Mission: The Growth of a Work of God* (1918; repr., Singapore: OMF, 1995), 175.
15. Pollock, *Keswick Story*, 16.

ter's prayer room. He was Trumbull's right-hand man until McQuilkin became the founder and president of Columbia Bible School in 1923.

3. WHAT ARE SOME INFLUENTIAL VARIATIONS ON HIGHER LIFE THEOLOGY?

Higher life theology spawned four institutions or movements that have greatly influenced American evangelicalism: the Christian and Missionary Alliance, Moody Bible Institute, Pentecostalism, and Dallas Theological Seminary. Those four successors to higher life theology each began as influential variations on higher life theology (emphasis on *began as*—today the Christian and Missionary Alliance, Moody Bible Institute, and Dallas Theological Seminary do not promote higher life theology like they used to).

THE CHRISTIAN AND MISSIONARY ALLIANCE: FOUNDED BY A. B. SIMPSON

A. B. Simpson (1844-1919) founded two nondenominational mission agencies in 1887 that merged in 1897 as the Christian and Missionary Alliance. It was not technically part of the higher life movement but was sympathetic with it. Simpson, who authored over one hundred books, experienced his higher life crisis in 1874 when reading Boardman's *The Higher Christian Life*. His view of sanctification was similar but not identical to the Wesleyan and Keswick views.[16] He viewed sanctification as the Christ-filled life, which begins at a crisis that occurs at a point in time after one has already become a Christian. At this crisis, a Christian is filled or baptized with the Holy Spirit. But unlike Pentecostalism, Simpson did not believe that speaking in tongues is an evidence of that crisis.

---

16. William C. Kostlevy, "Simpson, A(lbert) B(enjamin)," in *Historical Dictionary of the Holiness Movement*, ed. William C. Kostlevy (Lanham, MD: Scarecrow, 2001), 233: "Rejecting both the Wesleyan teaching that the sinful nature is eradicated in sanctification and the Keswick notion that the sinful nature is suppressed, Simpson, drawing on the Catholic mystical tradition of Madame Guyon (1648-1717) and Francis Fénelon (1651-1715), insisted that the point of sanctification was the life of Christ in the believer."

MOODY BIBLE INSTITUTE:
LED BY D. L. MOODY, R. A. TORREY, AND JAMES M. GRAY

Moody Bible Institute began in 1889 as the Bible Institute for Home and Foreign Missions of the Chicago Evangelization Society. In March 1900 (after Moody's death in December 1899), its name changed to Moody Bible Institute. It emphasized practical Christian ministry, and it became an internationally influential force in evangelicalism through its faculty, graduates, and ministries such as Moody Press. Moody Bible Institute's first three leaders enthusiastically spread elements of higher life theology.

1. *D. L. Moody* (1837–1899) emphasized that Christians must experience a crisis of Spirit-baptism after their conversion. He testified that he received the baptism of the Spirit just after the great Chicago fire in 1871 while walking on Wall Street in New York City. Although Moody never entirely or exclusively embraced higher life theology, he was publicly sympathetic with it and allowed it to spread at his popular Northfield Conferences.[17] He passionately emphasized that Christians should be baptized with the Holy Spirit in order to have power to serve God and others. Other leaders who followed Moody by emphasizing Spirit-baptism or Spirit-filling as the key for "power for service" include A. J. Gordon, A. T. Pierson, C. I. Scofield, R. A. Torrey, and James M. Gray.

2. *R. A. Torrey* (1856–1928) was superintendent of Moody Bible Institute (1889–1908) and laid the foundation for its curriculum. He was one of Moody's closest friends and pastored Chicago Avenue Church (1894–1906), which the church renamed Moody Church in 1908. Torrey shared speaking platforms in America with many Keswick speakers, such as F. B. Meyer, and he spoke at the Keswick Convention in 1904 on his most passionate subject: how to receive the baptism of the Spirit. Torrey further accented what Moody emphasized: Spirit-baptism is a crisis that occurs after a person is

---

17. Moody's theology was as broad as possible within evangelicalism. "Moody would never have identified exclusively with one strand of teaching." Ian M. Randall, "A Christian Cosmopolitan: F. B. Meyer in Britain and America," in *Amazing Grace: Evangelicalism in Australia, Britain, Canada, and the United States*, ed. George A. Rawlyk and Mark A. Noll (Grand Rapids: Baker Books, 1993), 166.

already a Christian, and it results in power for service. Early Pentecostal literature quotes Torrey more frequently than it quotes any other non-Pentecostal.

3. *James M. Gray* (1851–1935) began lecturing at Moody Bible Institute in 1892 and remained there until his death. He served as dean (1904–1923), president (1923–1934), and president emeritus. He was sympathetic with Moody and Torrey's view of sanctification, but he did not view Spirit-baptism as a separate experience that occurs after conversion. He emphasized Spirit-filling as the secret key to victorious living and Spirit-anointing as the means for power in service.

PENTECOSTALISM: A PRODUCT OF WESLEYAN PERFECTIONISM, THE HOLINESS MOVEMENT, HIGHER LIFE THEOLOGY, A. B. SIMPSON, D. L. MOODY, AND R. A. TORREY

Pentecostalism, according to most church historians, began on December 31, 1900. Charles Fox Parham (1873–1929), a teacher at Bethel Bible School in Topeka, Kansas, laid his hands on Miss Agnes Ozman that day, and she soon began speaking in tongues. Within days, Parham and many other students also experienced what they believed was the initial evidence of Spirit-baptism.

Pentecostalism maintains that believers should experience Spirit-baptism after conversion and initially demonstrate this by speaking in tongues. Pentecostals are divided regarding whether Spirit-baptism happens at the sanctification crisis or at a later time. Thus, some call Spirit-baptism "the second blessing" (see fig. 2.3) and others "the third blessing." The three blessings are (1) the crisis of conversion for salvation, (2) the crisis of sanctification for holiness, and (3) the crisis of Spirit-baptism for power in service (see fig. 1.3).

Pentecostalism's roots include Wesleyan perfectionism (Wesley, Fletcher, and Clarke), Methodist perfectionism (Palmer and the camp meetings), Oberlin perfectionism (Finney and Mahan), the higher life movement (Boardman and the Smiths), the early Keswick movement (especially F. B. Meyer, Andrew Murray, A. T. Pierson, and A. J. Gordon), and the theology of A. B. Simpson, D. L. Moody, and R. A. Torrey. Common to all these leaders and movements is affirming two distinct crisis events—one for conversion and one for a special sanctification. Higher life theology played a crucial role in forming Pentecostalism, which subsequently dwarfed higher life theology in size and influence.

Fig. 1.3. The Pentecostal View of Sanctification

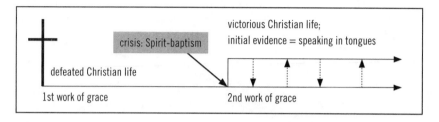

The figure contains text labels: "victorious Christian life; initial evidence = speaking in tongues", "crisis: Spirit-baptism", "defeated Christian life", "1st work of grace", "2nd work of grace"

DALLAS THEOLOGICAL SEMINARY:
BASTION OF THE CHAFERIAN VIEW OF SANCTIFICATION

The higher life and Chaferian views of sanctification are similar but not identical. The higher life view predated and highly influenced the Chaferian view, named after Lewis Sperry Chafer, who cofounded Dallas Theological Seminary in 1924.[18] Dallas Theological Seminary is probably the most influential factor for the prevalence of a Keswick-like view of sanctification in modern evangelicalism. Three theologians have been most influential:

1. *Lewis Sperry Chafer* (1871–1952) was the protégé of C. I. Scofield (1843–1921). After Scofield died, his former church in Dallas called Chafer to pastor them; Chafer accepted, and the church changed its name to Scofield Memorial Church. You cannot understand Chafer apart from Scofield.

   Scofield embraced higher life theology, and his famous *Scofield Reference Bible* "more or less canonized Keswick teachings."[19] Believers are in one of two distinct categories: (1) those who are not Spirit-filled and (2) those who are Spirit-filled. The first are

---

18. See the first book-length history of Dallas Theological Seminary: John D. Hannah, *An Uncommon Union: Dallas Theological Seminary and American Evangelicalism* (Grand Rapids: Zondervan, 2009).

19. George M. Marsden, *Fundamentalism and American Culture*, 2nd ed. (Oxford: Oxford University Press, 2006), 79.

powerless, and the second are powerful. But unlike Moody, Torrey, and Meyer, he insisted that Spirit-baptism occurs at conversion for all Christians.

In 1924, Chafer cofounded Dallas Theological Seminary (called Evangelical Theological College until 1936). He cofounded it with W. H. Griffith Thomas, one of the early Keswick movement's leaders. For the previous decade, Chafer had been contemplating the need for a seminary sympathetic with the Bible conference movement's teaching, especially higher life theology.[20] Although Chafer had earned no formal theological degrees, he served as both the school's president and professor of systematic theology from 1924 until his death in 1952.

At the beginning of each school year, Chafer presented a series of lectures on consecration as the prerequisite for the seminarians to be effective in their studies. He also taught a course on this subject entitled "Realization of the Spiritual Life" as part of the theological curriculum for first-year students. His lectures promoted higher life theology, and the essence of his lectures is in his book *He That Is Spiritual*, which "became popularly known as Victorious Life Teaching or Keswick Theology."[21] He opens his book by delineating three distinct categories into which all humans fall:

1. natural (unconverted)
2. carnal (converted but characterized by an unconverted lifestyle)
3. spiritual (converted and Spirit-filled)

People may experience "two great spiritual changes"—"the change from the 'natural' man to the saved man, and the change from the 'carnal' man to the 'spiritual' man."[22] "By various terms

---

20. Chafer did not call it "higher life theology," but what he taught was basically what I call higher life theology in this book. Chafer clarifies that he does not value "such man-made, unbiblical terms as 'second blessing,' 'a second work of grace,' 'the higher life,' and various phrases used in the perverted statements of the doctrines of sanctification and perfection." Lewis Sperry Chafer, *He That Is Spiritual* (Wheaton, IL: Van Kampen, 1918), 41.
21. Hannah, *Uncommon Union*, 85.
22. Chafer, *He That Is Spiritual*, 3, 13.

the Bible teaches that there are two classes of Christians." Figure 1.4 records Chafer's contrasts verbatim,[23] and figure 1.5 depicts the Chaferian view of sanctification.

Fig. 1.4. Chafer's Two Categories of Christians: Carnal and Spiritual

Category 1: Carnal	Category 2: Spiritual
Those who "abide not"	Those who "abide in Christ"
Those who "walk in darkness"	Those who are "walking in the light"
Those who "walk as men"	Those who "walk by the Spirit"
Those who "walk after the flesh"	Those who "walk in newness of life"
Those who have the Spirit "*in*" them, but not "*upon*" them	Those who have the Spirit "*in*" and "*upon*" them
Those who are "carnal"	Those who are "spiritual"
Those who are not ["filled with the Spirit"]	Those who are "filled with the Spirit"

Fig. 1.5. The Chaferian View of Sanctification

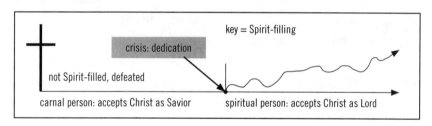

2. *John F. Walvoord* (1910-2002) served in leadership roles at Dallas Theological Seminary from 1935 until his death.[24] He perpetuated Chafer's Keswick-like view of sanctification. Carnal believ-

---

23. Ibid., 39.

24. Acting registrar (1935), registrar (1936-1945), associate professor of systematic theology (1936-1952), secretary of the faculty (1940-1945), assistant to the president (1945-1952), president (1953-1986), professor of systematic theology (1953-1986), editor of *Bibliotheca Sacra* (1952-1985), coeditor of *The Bible Knowledge Commentary* by Dallas Theological Seminary faculty (NT, 1983; OT, 1985), chancellor (1986-2001), and chancellor emeritus (2001-2002).

ers must surrender "once and for all" by accepting Christ "as Lord," resulting in the start of "progressive sanctification." He agrees with the Keswick perspective in *Five Views on Sanctification*, but qualifies that the only point that could use more clarity is to distinguish Spirit-baptism as a once-for-all-time act at conversion and Spirit-filling as the secret "means of transforming the Christian life."[25]

3. *Charles C. Ryrie* (1925-2016) "dedicated" his life to God after he met with Chafer on April 23, 1943. He later taught systematic theology at Dallas Theological Seminary (1953-1958), served as president of the Philadelphia College of the Bible (1958-1962), and returned to Dallas Theological Seminary to serve as chair of the systematic theology department and dean of doctoral studies until he retired (1962-1983).

    Like Walvoord, Ryrie promoted a Keswick-like view of sanctification by emphasizing "dedication," a once-for-all-time crisis that is never repeated and transitions believers from being carnal to spiritual.[26] He views the "Let go and let God" slogan as a quietistic, improper emphasis for the Christian life in general because "in the matter of progressive sanctification there is a part that the believer plays which he very definitely must not let go of." But the slogan "is a perfectly proper emphasis when it concerns the matter of dedication."[27]

    Ryrie contrasts Spirit-filling with Spirit-baptism in seven ways (see fig. 1.6).

---

25. John F. Walvoord, "Response to McQuilkin," in *Five Views on Sanctification*, ed. Stanley N. Gundry, Counterpoints (Grand Rapids: Zondervan, 1987), 194-95.
26. Ryrie, *Balancing the Christian Life*, 66, 77-86, 184-96. See also Ryrie, "Contrasting Views on Sanctification," in *Walvoord: A Tribute*, ed. Donald K. Campbell (Chicago: Moody, 1982), 189-200.
27. Ryrie, *Balancing the Christian Life*, 66.

Fig. 1.6. Ryrie's Contrast between Spirit-Baptism and Spirit-Filling[28]

Baptism [of the Spirit]	Filling [of the Spirit]
Occurs only once in each believer's life	Is a repeated experience
Never happened before day of Pentecost	Occurred in the Old Testament
True of all believers	Not necessarily experienced by all
Cannot be undone	Can be lost
Results in a POSITION	Results in POWER
Occurs when we believe in Christ	Occurs throughout the Christian life
No prerequisite (except faith in Christ)	Depends on yieldedness

The Chaferian view of sanctification is directly related to the so-called Lordship salvation controversy.[29] The controversy in 1919 between Chafer (Chaferian) and Warfield (Reformed) repeated itself in the 1950s with Steven Barabas (Keswick) and John Murray (Reformed) and again in the late 1980s and the 1990s with Ryrie (Chaferian) and John MacArthur (Reformed). Ryrie's chapter "Must Christ Be Lord to Be Savior?" answers the question with a dogmatic *No*:

> The importance of this question cannot be overestimated in relation to both salvation and sanctification. The message of faith only and the message of faith plus commitment of life

---

28. Ibid., 119. This reproduces Ryrie's table.

29. I say "so-called" because the label is unhelpful. I agree with Wayne Grudem, *"Free Grace" Theology: 5 Ways It Diminishes the Gospel* (Wheaton, IL: Crossway, 2016), 22–24: "The phrase *Lordship salvation* [is] a decidedly misleading and unfortunate summary of the central issues involved. ... Both sides agree that Jesus is Lord of our lives in some sense and is not fully Lord of our lives in another sense. Trying to define precisely how much Jesus has to be acknowledged as Lord for genuine saving faith becomes an increasingly muddled task .... My own conclusion is that there are important differences concerning two other matters: 1) whether repentance from sin (in the sense of remorse for sin and an internal resolve to forsake it) is necessary for saving faith, and 2) whether good works and continuing to believe necessarily follow from saving faith. The two positions clearly and explicitly disagree on the answers to those questions. And it is on those two questions that the debate should be focused."

cannot both be the gospel; therefore, one of them is a false gospel and comes under the curse of perverting the gospel or preaching another gospel (Gal 1:6–9), and this is a very serious matter. As far as sanctification is concerned, if only committed people are saved people, then where is there room for carnal Christians?[30]

The controversy erupted again in 1988 with MacArthur's *The Gospel according to Jesus*.[31] Zane Hodges and Ryrie each responded to MacArthur,[32] and MacArthur responded to Hodges and Ryrie.[33] MacArthur's first work argues that the Gospels teach that one must repent to be saved and that good works and continuing to believe in Jesus are the necessary fruit of saving faith, and Hodges argues that neither the Gospels nor the rest of the Bible supports that. Hodges contends that the only condition for salvation is intellectually believing and that other elements such as repentance and surrender are heretical additions to the gospel that result in salvation by works rather than by faith alone. Hodges denies that a person who believes in Christ must continue believing to possess eternal life—someone who previously believed in Christ can "drop out" of the Christian life, just as a student can drop out of school.[34]

Ryrie, though not as extreme as Hodges, also argues that neither the Gospels nor the rest of the Bible supports that one must repent to be saved or that good works and continuing to believe in Jesus are the necessary fruit of saving faith. His main argument is that God requires only that people *believe* in Jesus Christ for him to save them. He argues that Christians may be in a lifelong state of carnality and may even become unbelieving believ-

---

30. Ryrie, *Balancing the Christian Life*, 178.

31. John MacArthur, *The Gospel according to Jesus: What Is Authentic Faith?*, 3rd ed. (Grand Rapids: Zondervan, 2008). See John Piper, "Putting God Back into Faith: Review of John MacArthur's *The Gospel According to Jesus*," in vol. 12 of *The Collected Works of John Piper*, ed. David Mathis and Justin Taylor (Wheaton, IL: Crossway, 2017), 333–37.

32. Zane C. Hodges, *Absolutely Free! A Biblical Reply to Lordship Salvation* (Dallas: Zondervan, 1989); Charles C. Ryrie, *So Great Salvation: What It Means to Believe in Jesus Christ* (Wheaton, IL: Victor, 1989).

33. John MacArthur, *Faith Works: The Gospel according to the Apostles* (Dallas: Word, 1993).

34. Hodges, *Absolutely Free!*, 80–82, 104, 111–12, etc.

ers; those who once believed are secure forever—even if they turn away.[35] Hodges and Ryrie distinguish between salvation and discipleship based on how Chafer adopted and adapted the categories of carnal and spiritual Christians from higher life theology.[36]

These debates have continued within evangelicalism. More recently, Wayne Grudem and John MacArthur (once again) have helpfully addressed this controversial issue.[37]

CONCLUSION

This chapter has been a short way of telling the story of higher life theology—where it came from, who initially popularized it, and four influential variations on it. It is important to understand this story before critiquing higher life theology.

But before we begin to critique it, we must answer one more question: What exactly is higher life theology? The next chapter explains its essence.

---

35. Ryrie, *So Great Salvation*, 59–66, 141, 143.
36. Donald Louis Ketcham, "The Lordship Salvation Debate: Its Nature, Causes, and Significance" (PhD diss., Baylor University, 1995), 328, 343–47.
37. Grudem, *"Free Grace" Theology*; John MacArthur, *The Gospel according to Paul: Embracing the Good News at the Heart of Paul's Teachings* (Nashville: Nelson, 2017).

CHAPTER 2

What Is Higher Life Theology?

We will evaluate higher life theology in chapters 3–4, but before we can do that, we must know what it is. One helpful way to explain higher life theology is to present it in five steps. These five steps correspond to the five days of sequential, progressive teaching at a typical early Keswick Convention (see fig. 2.1). A week at a Keswick Convention focused on the Bible and Christian fellowship. It was supposed to be like a spiritual resort—or more accurately, like a spiritual hospital. One leading Keswick historian describes those weeklong Keswick meetings as "a spiritual clinic" to help restore Christians who were spiritually sick or wounded.[1]

Fig. 2.1. "A Spiritual Clinic": The Early Keswick Convention's Progressive Teaching

Day 1: Monday	Day 2: Tuesday	Day 3: Wednesday	Day 4: Thursday	Day 5: Friday
The diagnosis: sin	The cure: God's provision for victorious Christian living	The crisis for the cure: consecration	The prescription: Spirit-filling	The mission: powerful Christian service (especially foreign missions)

Everything this chapter asserts is what higher life theology affirms. Even the illustrations come directly from higher life teaching. (It would get tire-

---

1. Steven Barabas, *So Great Salvation: The History and Message of the Keswick Convention* (Westwood, NJ: Revell, 1952), 30.

some to keep repeating phrases such as "According to higher life theology.") This chapter presents higher life theology without evaluating it; chapters 3 and 4 evaluate it.

DAY 1. THE DIAGNOSIS: SIN

Sin is why some Christians are spiritually sick or wounded. Sin is an indwelling tendency or law, and you can't eradicate it in this life. The only way to conquer sin is to continually counteract it; the only law that can counteract the law of sin in the Christian (Rom 7:23) is the law of the Spirit in Christ (Rom 8:2); and the only way for the law of the Spirit in Christ to counteract the law of sin in the Christian is for the Christian to abide in Christ. Figure 2.2 summarizes several illustrations that higher life teachers use to clarify this "law of counteraction."

It is not possible to be sinlessly perfect, but it is possible to live without "known sin." The decisive factor in successfully counteracting sin is whether you allow the Holy Spirit to counteract your sinful nature. "Christians need not sin, and if they allow the Holy Spirit to 'operate invariably' they will not sin."[2]

DAY 2. THE CURE: GOD'S PROVISION FOR VICTORIOUS CHRISTIAN LIVING

FUNDAMENTAL PROPOSITION:
THERE ARE TWO CATEGORIES OF CHRISTIANS

The cure for sin is based on the fundamental proposition that there are two categories of Christians (see fig. 2.3, which uses higher life theology's own labels).

---

2. W. H. Griffith Thomas, "The Victorious Life (I.)," *Bibliotheca Sacra* 76 (1919): 275.

Fig. 2.2. Illustrations of Counteracting Sin

The law of sin in the Christian	The law of the Spirit in Christ	The law of counteraction
Dark room	Light from a candle	Light counteracts darkness only when the light abides in the dark room.
A rod attached to lead sinks in a tank of water.	The rod floats in a little life-belt.	The life-belt counteracts sinking only when the rod abides in the life-belt.
A man in the sea would eventually sink to the bottom.	The man in a life-belt would float on the surface.	The life-belt counteracts sinking only when a man abides in the life-belt.
Peter sinks when trying to walk on water.	Peter walks on water through Christ's power.	Christ's power counteracts sinking only when Peter gazes on Christ.
A hot-air balloon without gas rests on the ground.	The hot-air balloon soars above the ground when hot gas inflates it.	The hot gas counteracts gravity's effect on the hot-air balloon only when the gas abides in the balloon.
Iron by itself is black, cold, and hard.	Iron in the fire is red, hot, and malleable because the fire is in the iron.	Fire counteracts iron's blackness, coldness, and hardness only when the iron abides in the fire.
A particular young lion is savage and blood-thirsty.	The lion is tame when in the presence of its keeper.	The keeper counteracts the lion's savage nature only when the keeper abides in the lion's presence.

Fig. 2.3. Two Categories of Christians

Category 1	Category 2
Carnal	Spiritual
Justified but no crisis of sanctification	Justified and crisis of sanctification
Justification actual (factual); sanctification possible	Sanctification actual and experiential (functional)
Received Christ by faith as your righteousness	Received Christ by faith as your holiness
Free from sin's penalty	Free from sin's power
First blessing	Second blessing (followed by more blessings)
First stage	Second stage
Average	Normal
Constant defeat	Constant victory
Expect defeat, surprised by victory	Expect victory, surprised by defeat
Life in the flesh	Life in the Spirit
Not abiding in Christ	Abiding in Christ
Have life	Have life more abundantly
Spirit-indwelt	Spirit-baptized and Spirit-filled
Spirit-indwelt	Christ-indwelt
Christ is Savior	Christ is both Savior and Lord
Believer	Disciple
Out of fellowship/ communion with God	In fellowship/communion with God
Headship: "in Christ" positionally	Fellowship: "in Christ" experientially
The self-life (Rom 7)	The Christ-life (Rom 8)
Spiritual bondage	Spiritual liberty
Duty-life	Love-life
Restless worry	Perfect peace and rest
Experientially pre-Pentecost	Experientially post-Pentecost
No power for service	Power for service
Virtual fruitlessness	Abundant fruitfulness

Category 1	Category 2
Stagnation	Perpetual freshness
Feebleness	Strength
Lower life	Higher life
Shallow life	Deeper life
Trying	Trusting
The life of struggle/works	The life/rest of faith
The unsurrendered life	The life of consecration
The life lacking blessing	The blessed life
Liberated from Egypt but still in the wilderness	In the land of Canaan
The Christian life as it ought not be	The Christian life as it ought to be

There are three distinct types of people:

1. Non-Christian (natural)
2. Christian in category 1 (carnal)
3. Christian in category 2 (spiritual)

The way to help non-Christians is to evangelize them so they convert and become Christians. The way to help Christians in category 1 is to teach them higher life theology so they experience a crisis that moves them from category 1 to category 2. That crisis or "second blessing" for the Christian is sometimes "as clearly marked as his conversion, in which he passes out of a life of continual feebleness and failure to one of strength and victory, and abiding rest."[3] This experience "has been called by various names": "the second blessing" (Wesley), "the higher Christian life" (Boardman), "the rest of faith," "the life of consecration," "the life of faith," and "the blessed life." But it is simply *the Christian life, as it ought to be, but seldom is.*"[4] If

---

3. Andrew Murray, *The Two Covenants and the Second Blessing* (New York: Revell, 1898), 168–69.

4. J. Elder Cumming, "What We Teach," in *Keswick's Triumphant Voice: Forty-Eight Outstanding Addresses Delivered at the Keswick Convention, 1883–1962*, ed. Herbert F. Stevenson (Grand Rapids: Zondervan, 1963), 19.

you don't understand higher life theology, you can't move from category 1 to category 2.[5]

PROBLEM: WRONG VIEWS ON SANCTIFICATION RESULT IN DEFEAT (CATEGORY 1)

Defeat (i.e., category 1) characterizes the "average" Christian—largely because they believe wrong views on sanctification. Here are three of those wrong views.

1. *Automatic growth.* Sanctification is not automatic. Believers do not automatically progress in sanctification like programmed robots. This view insufficiently accounts for Christian backsliding.

2. *Synergism.* This view of sanctification is incorrect because it claims a Christian grows by diligently using the means of grace with God's help—that is, both God and the believer work. But God does everything and the believer does nothing. The believer's own strength is not only insufficient for sanctification; depending on that strength offends God.[6]

---

5. Charles G. Trumbull, *Victory in Christ: Messages on the Victorious Life* (repr., Fort Washington, PA: Christian Literature Crusade, 2000), 9: "Jesus, you know, makes two offers to everyone. He offers to set us free from the *penalty* of our sin. And He offers to set us free from the *power* of our sin. Both these offers are made on exactly the same terms: we can accept them only by letting Him do it all. Every Christian has accepted the first offer. Many Christians have not accepted the second offer." J. Elder Cumming, *Through the Eternal Spirit* (Chicago: Revell, 1896), 109: "It is admitted by all that there is a great difference in experience between a Christian who merely has the 'new life' and one who has it 'more abundantly.' The former may not even be sure that he is a Christian at all, and his friends may also doubt it; but the latter is full of joy, and overflows with blessing. The former is merely a *converted* man, the latter is a *sanctified* man, and there is a gulf between them."

6. Cumming, *Through the Eternal Spirit*, 157-58: "A third misapprehension about sanctification is that it is to be gained by our own personal efforts—by *working for it*. We make it our aim. We do all we can to bring it about. We use the means, and it does not come. Great is the bondage into which many fall, and in which they continue for years, by this unceasing effort to become godly, and by its fruitlessness. ... Growth is not the product of effort, but of life. Neither a tree nor a man grows by effort. ... One more mistake into which men fall is to suppose that the work of sanctification *must be shared between God and them*. We make the effort, and we ask God to bless it. Nay, we go a step farther, and request God to *help* us to be holy, which obviously means that we should do part, and that God should come in to complete

3. *Eradication of the law of indwelling sin.* Both the Wesleyan view (i.e., God completely and instantaneously eradicates the indwelling sin tendency) and the Reformed view (i.e., a Christian gradually mortifies sin but not completely until glorification) are wrong. A Christian does not gradually become less sinful; sin is an indwelling tendency that does not change. Like a barrel of dry gunpowder that could explode at any moment under the right conditions, as a Christian you can fall into the same kind of sin at any moment of your life—whether you just converted or have been a Christian for seventy years.[7]

SOLUTION: SANCTIFICATION BY FAITH RESULTS IN VICTORY (CATEGORY 2)

The correct view is "sanctification by faith," which results in victory (i.e., category 2). Defeat characterizes the "average" Christian, but victory characterizes the "normal" Christian. (Sanctification refers to what happens starting at the crisis. See fig. 2.4.)

Fig. 2.4. The Higher Life (or Keswick) View of Sanctification

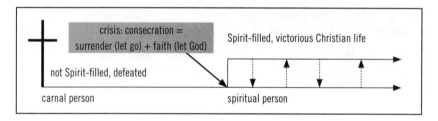

It helps to specify sanctification's basis, nature, means, result, and agent.

1. *On what basis?* The *basis* for sanctification is union with Christ. The key text is Romans 6. All believers are positionally united to Christ, so it is *possible* for them to live the victorious Christian life.

---

the work, and do that part of it which we cannot fully do. ... This is a different case from growing in holiness, where God must do the whole or nothing; where He will not share the work with us, much less do the smaller part of it."

7. Thomas, "The Victorious Life (I.)," 273–74.

2. *What is it?* The *nature* of sanctification is threefold: (1) gift, (2) crisis, and (3) process. Sanctification is a gift that a believer must willingly receive. It begins with the crisis of consecration, and what follows is a process (see fig. 2.5).

Fig. 2.5. Illustrations of Sanctification as a Crisis Followed by a Process

Crisis	Process
The beginning point of a line	The rest of the line
Stepping onto a train	Traveling on a train
Matriculating into a school	Receiving instruction at the school
Taking a photograph	Developing the photograph
Setting a dislocated ankle with instant relief	Walking with the healed ankle
Enthroning a king	The king ruling
While wrestling with the Lord, Jacob ceased resisting (i.e., he yielded or surrendered or "let go"), and he clung to the Lord for a blessing (i.e., he exercised faith or "let God").	Jacob (now Israel) lived honestly rather than deceptively.
The Israelites crossing the Jordan River	The Israelites living in the land of Canaan
Jesus completely, immediately cured people.	Those people remained cured.
Peter wept bitterly after denying the Lord.	Peter began living a powerful Christian life.

Believers must experience the crisis before the process can begin. The Greek word translated "present" in Romans 6:13, 16, 19, and 12:1 is in the aorist tense-form, which supports that this "presenting" is a once-for-all-time act of self-surrender. But Christians may need to repeat that yielding "if, having presented ourselves, we have afterwards withdrawn the gift."[8] "The act of consecration"

---

8. Evan H. Hopkins, *The Law of Liberty in the Spiritual Life* (1920; repr., Fort Washington, PA: Christian Literature Crusade, 1991), 95.

is "done once for all" but still must "be done over and over again" "*in the sense of restoration*" or "*confirmation*."[9] This yielding is not necessary for justification, but it is necessary for sanctification. Christians often make this decisive step of yielding immediately after hearing a sermon on the crisis of sanctification.[10]

3. *How?* The *means* of sanctification is appropriating (i.e., choosing to make use of) the gift by faith alone—not by effort or struggle. Popular phrases for this concept are "sanctification by faith" and "holiness by faith." Figure 2.6 illustrates the difference between a Christian's (a) having a position and (b) appropriating that position.

Fig. 2.6. Illustrations of Appropriating the Gift of Sanctification

Having a Position (Sanctification Is Possible)	Appropriating That Position (Sanctification Is Actual)
You live as if you are poor even though you have a large checking account.	Live as if you are rich by using your wealth.
You are enslaved even though the government has proclaimed you are free.	Become free by acting on what the government proclaimed.
The nobleman *sought* Jesus to heal his son ("seeking faith").	The nobleman *believed* that Jesus had healed his son ("resting faith").
You own a large estate but don't know about the treasures beneath the surface (e.g., mineral wealth).	Discover and use the wealth you already possess.

9. Evan H. Hopkins, "Crisis and Process," in *Keswick's Authentic Voice: Sixty-Five Dynamic Addresses Delivered at the Keswick Convention, 1875–1957*, ed. Herbert F. Stevenson (Grand Rapids: Zondervan, 1959), 336.

10. Cumming, "What We Teach," 25: "All Christians are urged to take such a step. An opportunity is often given by what is called an after-meeting, at a time when a solemn impression remains, when a favourable hour lingers before leaving; and then by a definite step of faith within the soul, and sometimes by an act of testimony visible to others, hundreds have passed from a lower to a higher stage of experience in the Christian life."

God will enable Christians to do what he commands, but unbelief limits God's enabling.[11] "The will is our main and chief impediment."[12] All Christians are united to Christ, but not all experience spiritual power because "the great hindrance—that which lies at the root of every other—is *unbelief*. We limit God by our unbelief."[13] Christians are unable to deliver themselves, and God is unable to deliver Christians unless they freely choose for God to deliver them. Trumbull compares it to conversion: "God can save no man unless that man does his part toward salvation." That is, a human's will must "voluntarily and deliberately decide to take what God offers us."[14] And once a Christian appropriates their position and makes sanctification actual, their free will is the only instrument that can keep allowing God to deliver them.[15]

4. *With what result?* The *result* of sanctification is spiritual power. All Christians are united to Christ, but they must appropriate spiritual power through faith. When a Christian's faith increases, "the power will flow in."[16] Christians without the power of the Holy

---

11. F. B. Meyer, *Christian Living* (London: Morgan & Scott, 1900), 62, 77: "'Wilt thou be made whole?' The whole question turns on the attitude of the will. ... *Wilt* thou be made whole? Christ asks that question of thee, my reader. Is not the Holy Spirit producing in thee a holy willingness? If so, tell thy Saviour so. He wills; *wilt* thou? If thou dost, then He undertakes to do all the rest; producing in thee health and life, wholeness and everlasting joy."

12. F. B. Meyer, *The Christ-Life for the Self-Life* (Chicago: Bible Institute Colportage Association, 1897), 42.

13. Hopkins, *Law of Liberty*, 127. Although "all Christians have Christ, and possess therefore all the resources of spiritual power and abundant fruitfulness," many believers remain defeated because they do not appropriate the gift of sanctification by faith. "Christ has power to overcome this hindrance" of the unbelief of believers, but that is not "the method of His working" nor "the law of His dealing with men"; a human's will must remain free. "We have limited the Holy One by our unbelief. We have 'set a mark' on the extent of His power to overcome and deliver, to keep and to save" (111–12).

14. Trumbull, *Victory in Christ*, 47.

15. Ibid., 13: "This miracle is sustained and continued in our life only by our continuing, moment-by-moment faith in our Saviour for his moment-by-moment victory over the power of our sin."

16. Hopkins, *Law of Liberty*, 127.

Spirit are like a train without an engine or like a power tool without electricity.

5. *By whom?* The *agent* of sanctification is the Holy Spirit, who imparts Christ to the believer. The Holy Spirit opposes a Christian's other indwelling power: the flesh (Gal 5:16–18).

DAY 3. THE CRISIS FOR THE CURE: CONSECRATION

"No crisis before Wednesday" was a common saying at the early Keswick Conventions because the first two days (Monday and Tuesday) laid the groundwork for the crisis of consecration. Since sanctification is a crisis plus a following process, it is important to focus on how to experience the crisis so that the process may follow. "What are the conditions of this Victorious Life? Only two, and they are very simple. Surrender and faith. 'Let go, and let God.'"[17] Believers enter the higher life through a crisis experience—the "twin door" of "surrender and faith."[18]

STEP 1: "LET GO" (SURRENDER)

It is at this point in time that Christians completely give themselves to Jesus as their Master. "Letting go" includes surrendering to God every habit, ambition, hope, loved one, possession, as well as yourself.

> Any victory over the power of any sin whatsoever in your life that you have to get by working for it is counterfeit. Any victory that you have to get by trying for it is counterfeit. If you have to work for your victory, it is not the real thing; it is not the thing that God offers you.[19]

> It is not by straining and struggling that this blessed condition is brought about; it comes by a very real dedication of ourselves to God for this very purpose, and with this as the special end and aim in view. Just lie quietly before Him. Open all the avenues of your being, and let Him come in and take possession of every chamber. Especially give Him your

---

17. Trumbull, *Victory in Christ*, 14.
18. J. C. Pollock, *The Keswick Story: The Authorized History of the Keswick Convention* (Chicago: Moody, 1964), 74 (paraphrasing Moule).
19. Trumbull, *Victory in Christ*, 34–35.

heart—the very seat of your desires, the throne of your affections. Yield all up to Him, and the Lord will enter, bringing with Him all the riches of His grace and glory, turning your life of duty into a life of liberty and love.[20]

STEP 2: "LET GOD" (FAITH)

After you "let go," you must "let God." First you surrender, then you exercise faith.

The secret of complete victory is faith: simply believing that *Jesus has done and is doing it all.* Victory is entered upon by a single act of faith, as is salvation. Victory is maintained by the attitude of faith. But suppose the believer having experienced the miracle of victory over sin through trusting his Lord's sufficiency, comes, somehow, to doubt that sufficiency? At once his victory is broken, and he fails. This is possible at any moment. ... They say at Keswick, "If you *should* fail, shout Victory!" Not with any idea of denying the reality of the failure, but in recognition of the fact that *Jesus* has not failed, and that there may be instantaneous and complete restoration through faith in His unimpaired sufficiency.[21]

"LET GO" + "LET GOD" = CONSECRATION

Steps one and two combined (i.e., "let go" + "let God") equal "consecration." Only then can you experience victory over sin. Some Christians have neither "let go" nor "let God," and others have "let go" but not "let God." That second group is "sure to be defeated." But after you "let go *and* let God," God is obligated to keep you from sin's power.[22] The key is resting (not struggling) and "trusting" (not "trying").

If any of you are making the mistake of trying to live the victorious life, you are cheating yourself out of it, for the victory you get by trying for it is a counterfeit victory. You must

---

20. Hopkins, *Law of Liberty,* 87.
21. Trumbull, *Victory in Christ,* 84–85.
22. Ibid., 15: Christians "must know and remember that it at once becomes His responsibility, His—I say it reverently—duty, to keep you from the power of sin."

substitute another word; not try, but trust, and you cannot try and trust at the same time. Trying is what we do, and trusting is what we let the Lord do. ... The counterfeit victory means a struggle; whatever we do, we do by our efforts. Oh, yes, we ask Him to help us, and then we feel that we must do a lot to help Him—as if He needed to be helped! In real victory, He does it all. We do not dare to help. We realize that the battle is His.[23]

"*Our efforts*" not only play no part in victory, "*they can and do effectually prevent such victory.*"[24] When you exercise your free will to "let God," you are not exerting "effort."[25]

Consecration is a crisis that occurs instantaneously. Victory comes immediately, not gradually; it is an instantaneous gift. "A victory gained ... by a gradual conquest over evil, getting one sin after another out of our life, is *counterfeit* victory."[26] "The victorious life, the life of freedom from the power of sin, is not a gradual gift. There is no such thing as a gradual gift. And victory is a gift. It is not a growth. ... We only begin to grow normally, grow as God wants us to grow, after we have entered into victory."[27]

DAY 4. THE PRESCRIPTION: SPIRIT-FILLING

When you experience a crisis of consecration (i.e., you "let go" *and* "let God"), you are Spirit-filled. Continuing to be Spirit-filled is the only way to spiritually grow and to avoid relapsing to category 1 (see fig. 2.3). And the way to remain Spirit-filled is to continue to let go and let God.

IS SPIRIT-FILLING DIFFERENT THAN SPIRIT-BAPTISM?

Andrew Murray shared his personal testimony at the 1895 Keswick Convention:

Some of you have heard how I have pressed upon you the two stages in the Christian life, and the step from one to

---

23. Ibid., 35, 43.
24. Ibid., 48.
25. Ibid., 51–52.
26. Ibid., 36.
27. Ibid., 38–39.

the other. The first ten years of my spiritual life were spent manifestly on the lower stage. ... Later on, my mind became much exercised about the baptism of the Holy Spirit, and I gave myself to God as perfectly as I could to receive this baptism of the Spirit. Yet there was failure.[28]

Early Keswick proponents generally used "Spirit-filling" and "Spirit-baptism" terminology synonymously, but in the 1900s, Keswick proponents gradually began to use Spirit-baptism terminology for what all Christians experience when they first repent and believe and to reserve Spirit-filling terminology for what only some Christians experience at consecration. That helped distinguish the Keswick view from Wesleyanism and Pentecostalism (see chap. 1).

Who Can Experience Spirit-Filling?

All Christians have the Spirit, but not all Christians are Spirit-filled. Only *consecrated* Christians can be Spirit-filled. That is, only Christians who have experienced a crisis of consecration (i.e., they have "let go and let God") can be Spirit-filled.

The practical point is: have you ever claimed and received the power of the Holy Ghost as such? When he came down on Pentecost and filled disciples, this experience was both subsequent to and different from *conversion*. ... Grant that Pentecost was the filling of an exhaustless Reservoir for the Church of all ages, what is to hinder every one of us from being filled at that Reservoir, and so having our own individual Pentecost? ... The practical question remains, "Are you baptized with the Holy Ghost?"[29]

What Is Spirit-Filling?

In the command "Be filled with the Spirit" (Eph 5:18), the Spirit is the content of the filling. As water fills a container, so the Spirit fills a Christian (see fig. 2.7). But a Spirit-filled Christian must not "relapse" and experience

---

28. Cited in Barabas, *So Great Salvation*, 178, 180.
29. Arthur T. Pierson, *The Keswick Movement in Precept and Practice* (New York: Funk & Wagnalls, 1903), 82–83, 119.

"spiritual *leakage*."[30] That would require "a refilling."[31] There is no guarantee that a Christian who is Spirit-filled will remain Spirit-filled. Just as Christians must allow the Spirit to fill them initially, so Christians must continue to allow the Spirit to keep on filling them.[32]

Fig. 2.7. Illustrations of Spirit-Filling

Illustration	Explanation
A cup filled with water	The cup may be full, overflowing, or in periodic need of refilling because of leakage.
A person breathing in air	The same life-giving properties in the air are in that person.
Iron in the fire	Iron by itself is black, cold, and hard, but iron in the fire is red, hot, and malleable because the fire is in the iron.

---

30. Hopkins, *Law of Liberty*, 174: "The normal conditions of the believer may be illustrated by a vessel filled with water to the brim. This does not render him independent of further supplies, nor does it make him self-satisfied. On the contrary, to be thus 'full' is to be conscious of one's own utter insufficiency, and the necessity of God's sustaining and renewing grace, moment by moment. It is the soul who is 'full of the Holy Ghost' who really looks up, and trusts with childlike simplicity for the momentary supply. These 'fillings' come just when God sees they are needed; and then it is that the soul overflows with those 'rivers of living water' which our Lord declared should be characteristic of Pentecostal days. But the experience of so many of God's children is often sadly different. While they may know what it is at certain times to receive the fullness, and for a season to be 'full of the Holy Ghost,' so great and subtle is the spiritual *leakage* that, too commonly, it is not long before they relapse into a condition of emptiness, which renders them unfit for the Master's use."

31. F. B. Meyer, *Some Secrets of Christian Living* (London: Partridge, 1880), 42.

32. Cf. John MacNeil, *The Spirit-Filled Life* (Chicago: Bible Institute Colportage Association, 1896), 122–26.

What Are the Conditions and Results of Spirit-Filling?

Christians must meet specific conditions in order to be Spirit-filled.[33] Those conditions include consecration ("let go and let God"), confident appropriation, patience, holy desire, and cleansing from all known sin.[34]

The results of Spirit-filling include Christ-likeness, moral purity, deliverance from sin's power, power for service (especially evangelism), assurance of salvation, consciousness of Christ's presence, and detailed and direct guidance for decision-making.[35]

DAY 5. THE MISSION: POWERFUL CHRISTIAN SERVICE

Powerful Christian service follows from days 1–4. If Christians experience consecration and Spirit-filling, then they will serve God with power, especially by evangelizing non-Christians both at home and abroad (foreign missions).

CONCLUSION

Higher life theology asserts that there are two categories of Christians. The way for a Christian to move from "category 1" (i.e., carnal) to "category 2" (i.e., spiritual) is to "let go and let God." The crisis of consecration happens instantaneously, and the process of sanctification follows. Christians maintain that condition by continually allowing the Holy Spirit to fill them, which results in spiritual power.

That's what higher life theology is. Now that we have told the story of where it came from and explained what it is, we are ready to analyze it (part 2).

---

33. Barabas, *So Great Salvation*, 145: "Two things are crystal clear in Scripture; that not all Christians are filled with the Spirit, and that God commands all Christians to be filled with the Spirit. The responsibility is not God's, but that of believers. The condition of filling is also made crystal clear. In the words of the apostles, God gives the Holy Spirit to them that obey Him (Acts v. 32). The Holy Spirit can control our members only in so far as we allow Him to do so by our obedience. That is the only way the blessing of the fullness of the Spirit can be made experimental in our lives."
34. Keswick proponents present overlapping lists of conditions that believers must meet in order to be Spirit-filled. See Andrew David Naselli, *Let Go and Let God? A Survey and Analysis of Keswick Theology* (Bellingham, WA: Lexham, 2010), 209–12.
35. Keswick proponents present overlapping lists of the results of Spirit-filling. See ibid., 212–13.

PART 2

Why Higher Life Theology Is Harmful

Higher life theology is not all bad. It has at least five commendable characteristics:

1. *It exalts Christ.* It exhorts you to depend on Christ rather than yourself.

2. *It is warmly devotional.* It is better to be a God-loving, holiness-pursuing Christian who affirms higher life theology than a professing Christian who is theologically accurate but cold-hearted and immoral.[1]

> Whatever else Keswick's teaching may have gotten wrong, it was not wrong to say to all Christians that there is more joy, more peace, more love, more power, and more fruit to be enjoyed in Christ than we are presently enjoying. ... Any view of the Christian life that does not promote the desire for, and the pursuit of, this inexpressible fullness—this more—is as defective as the view that says its usual

---

1. Cf. D. A. Carson, *Showing the Spirit: A Theological Exposition of 1 Corinthians 12–14* (Grand Rapids: Baker Books, 1987), 160: "Although I think it extremely dangerous to pursue a second blessing attested by tongues, I think it is no less dangerous not to pant after God at all, and to be satisfied with a merely creedal Christianity that is kosher but complacent, orthodox but ossified, sound but soundly asleep." Albert N. Martin, *Living the Christian Life* (Carlisle, PA: Banner of Truth Trust, 1986), 28: "Frankly, I would rather be with a warm-hearted, woolly-headed 'Wesleyan' who thinks he needed and has had a second work of grace, but who is hungry for God, than the man who can sit for hours and prove that there is no such thing, and whose heart is as cold as a stone."

way of coming is through a single crisis experience of full consecration.[2]

3. *It emphasizes that Christians must practice spiritual disciplines.* It encourages Christians to read the Bible, pray, fellowship, hear and respond to preaching, and evangelize non-Christians locally and globally. And setting aside an entire week to focus on the Bible, fellowship, and rest is a recipe to refresh Christians.[3]

4. *It affirms fundamental orthodoxy.* It affirms the type of Bible teachings that are "of first importance" (1 Cor 15:3). Evangelical Christians have various views on progressive sanctification (see figs. 1.2, 1.3, 1.5, 2.4, and 3.8), but they have one view on the most core doctrines (e.g., the Trinity and justification by faith alone).[4] Higher life theology is not heresy—it does not deny core Bible teachings that are "of first importance."

5. *It has a legacy of faithful Christian leaders.* Many of the men who prominently spread higher life theology were sincere, devout, godly men who were above reproach, and they commendably desired that Christians be holy—that they walk by the Spirit and not gratify the desires of the flesh. Hudson Taylor was one of the most outstanding foreign missionaries in the modern missionary movement, and many of the writings of H. C. G. Moule and W. H.

---

2. John Piper, *A Camaraderie of Confidence: The Fruit of Unfailing Faith in the Lives of Charles Spurgeon, George Müller, and Hudson Taylor,* The Swans Are Not Silent (Wheaton, IL: Crossway, 2016), 86.

3. Simplicity characterized the atmosphere of Keswick Conventions. The conference leaders encouraged attendees to "lay aside for the time all reading except the Bible"; "avoid conversation which has a tendency to divert your mind from the object of the meetings"; and "eat moderately, dress simply, retire to rest early." A typical day at a Keswick Convention consisted of about six general meetings: an early morning prayer meeting; a Bible reading; worship meetings in the morning, afternoon, and evening; and an "after-meeting" after the evening worship meeting for further counsel. Steven Barabas, *So Great Salvation: The History and Message of the Keswick Convention* (Westwood, NJ: Revell, 1952), 36–37.

4. On how doctrines have levels of importance, see Andrew David Naselli, *How to Understand and Apply the New Testament: Twelve Steps from Exegesis to Theology* (Phillipsburg, NJ: P&R Publishing, 2017), 295–96.

Griffith Thomas—the best theologians of the early Keswick movement—are insightful.

> When we think of the honoured names which have been associated with Keswick like those of Handley Moule, Webb-Peploe, Andrew Murray, A. T. Pierson, we have to reckon with a movement which enlisted the support of cultured and devoted servants of Christ and one hesitates to embark upon criticism. But the cause neither of truth nor of love is promoted by suppressing warranted criticism.[5]

That last sentence transitions us from affirming higher life theology to critiquing it with "warranted criticism."

But how can higher life theology be so bad if godly Christians like Andrew Murray and Hudson Taylor believed it? Higher life theology commendably emphasizes that Christians must be holy and sacrificially serve God, but holy and fruitful living by no means distinguishes higher life theology from other views of progressive sanctification. All the major views on progressive sanctification have proponents who are exemplary, inspiring Christians. Disagreeing with a particular view of progressive sanctification in no way questions whether proponents are godly Christians.

The bottom line is that we shouldn't determine our view of the Christian life by counting up whom we perceive to be the most holy Christians and seeing which view has the most adherents. One factor is decisive: What does Scripture teach? As John Murray says, "The cause neither of truth nor of love is promoted by suppressing warranted criticism." So constructively criticizing a faulty view of progressive sanctification can actually advance the cause of truth and love. "Right thinking about the gospel produces right living in the gospel."[6]

---

5. John Murray, review of *So Great Salvation: The History and Message of the Keswick Convention*, by Steven Barabas, *Westminster Theological Journal* 16 (1953): 80.
6. Michael P. V. Barrett, *Complete in Him: A Guide to Understanding and Enjoying the Gospel*, 2nd ed. (Grand Rapids: Reformation Heritage, 2017), xiii, xiv, 20, 91, 161, 195, 208, 215, 267, 271.

So while I can affirm that higher life theology is not *all* bad, I still think it's harmful—for at least ten reasons.[7]

1. *Disjunction.* It creates two categories of Christians.
2. *A form of perfectionism.* It portrays a shallow and incomplete view of sin in the Christian life.
3. *A form of quietism.* It emphasizes passivity, not activity.
4. *A form of Pelagianism.* It portrays the Christian's free will as autonomously starting and stopping sanctification.
5. *Misreading.* It does not interpret and apply the Bible accurately.
6. *False Assurance.* It assures spurious "Christians" they are saved.
7. *Methodology.* It uses superficial formulas for instantaneous sanctification.
8. *Addiction.* It fosters dependency on experiences at special holiness meetings.
9. *Abuse.* It frustrates and disillusions the have-nots.
10. *Spin.* It misinterprets personal experiences.

The first reason is by far the most important. That's why it's the longest. It gets an entire chapter (chap. 3). Then the next chapter explains the other nine reasons (chap. 4).

---

7. I am focusing on the most compelling reasons. A less compelling reason, for example, is historical—higher life theology is a novel view of sanctification that is the offspring of Wesleyanism and the holiness movement.

CHAPTER 3

The Fundamental Reason Higher Life Theology Is Harmful

The fundamental reason higher life theology is harmful is that it creates two categories of Christians. It divides Christians into two distinct types (see fig. 2.3). This is the linchpin reason that higher life theology is wrong. Rather than addressing every contrast in figure 2.3, what follows addresses five of the most significant contrasts (see fig. 3.1).

Fig. 3.1. Higher Life Theology vs. the New Testament[1]

Higher Life Theology	The New Testament
Some Christians are justified but not being sanctified, and others are both justified and being sanctified.	All Christians are both justified and being sanctified.
Some Christians are carnal, and others are spiritual.	All Christians are spiritual; none are permanently carnal.
Some Christians are not Spirit-baptized, and others are Spirit-baptized.	All Christians are Spirit-baptized.
Some Christians are not Spirit-filled, and others are Spirit-filled.	All Christians are Spirit-filled to various degrees.
Some Christians do not abide in Christ, and others do abide in Christ.	All Christians abide in Christ to various degrees.

---

1. Framing the two views as (1) higher life theology and (2) the New Testament is obviously biased! That is shorthand for "how I understand the New Testament." The historical label for the view I think matches what the New Testament teaches is the Reformed view (see fig. 3.8).

The rest of this chapter unpacks those five contrasts.

1. ALL CHRISTIANS ARE BOTH JUSTIFIED AND BEING SANCTIFIED

The Bible uses three grammatical tenses for sanctification, and our focus here concerns the relationship of justification to *progressive* sanctification (see fig. 3.2):

Fig. 3.2. Three Tenses of Sanctification

Past	Present	Future
Definitive or positional sanctification (occurs simultaneously with conversion and justification)	Progressive sanctification	Perfect, complete, or final sanctification (i.e., glorification)
"I am (or *have been*) sanctified."	"I am being sanctified."	"I will be sanctified."
God sets a Christian apart from sin's penalty and their "old self" in Adam (Rom 6; Acts 20:32; 26:18; 1 Cor 1:2; 6:11; Heb 10:10, 14).	God gradually sets a Christian apart from sin's power and practice (John 17:17; 2 Cor 3:18; 7:1; Phil 1:6).	God sets a Christian apart from sin's presence and possibility (Phil 3:21; 1 Thess 3:12–13; Jude 24).

When the New Testament uses the holiness word-group (e.g., "holy" and "sanctify" or "make holy"), it usually refers to definitive sanctification rather than progressive sanctification.[2] But the *concept* of progressive sanctification permeates the New Testament. Progressive sanctification is "that gracious operation of the Holy Spirit, involving our responsible participation, by which he delivers us from the pollution of sin, renews our entire nature according to the image of God, and enables us to live lives that are pleasing to him."[3]

---

2. See David Peterson, *Possessed by God: A New Testament Theology of Sanctification and Holiness*, New Studies in Biblical Theology 1 (Downers Grove, IL: InterVarsity Press, 1995); Mark A. Snoeberger, "Definitive Sanctification: Threading a Path between Legal Fiction and Works Righteousness" (PhD diss., Baptist Bible Seminary, 2007); Andrew David Naselli, "Holiness," in *NIV Zondervan Study Bible*, ed. D. A. Carson (Grand Rapids: Zondervan, 2015), 2676–78.

3. Anthony A. Hoekema, *Saved by Grace* (Grand Rapids: Eerdmans, 1989), 192. Compare the answer to Question 35 in the Westminster Shorter Catechism: Progres-

Figure 3.3 contrasts justification and progressive sanctification:

**Fig. 3.3. Contrasts between Justification and
Progressive Sanctification**

	Justification	Progressive Sanctification
Quality	Instantly declared righteous	Gradually made righteous
	Objective, judicial (non-experiential): legal, forensic position	Subjective, experiential: daily experience
	External: outside the believer	Internal: inside the believer
	Christ's righteousness imputed, received judicially	Christ's righteousness imparted, worked out experientially
	Instantly removes sin's guilt and penalty	Gradually removes sin's pollution and power
	Does not change character	Gradually transforms character
Quantity	All Christians share the same legal standing	Christians are at different stages of growth
Duration	A single, instantaneous completed act: once-for-all-time, never repeated	A continuing process: gradual, maturing, lifelong

Progressive sanctification is distinct from justification yet *inseparable* from justification. Faith alone justifies, but the faith that justifies is never alone. God's grace through the power of his Spirit ensures that the same faith that justifies a Christian also sanctifies a Christian.

Higher life theology chronologically separates justification from progressive sanctification by emphasizing a crisis of consecration that occurs at a point in time *after* justification and enables progressive sanctification to begin. That essentially divides Christ as one whom people can "take" as their justifier (or Savior) without "taking" him as their sanctifier (or Lord).[4]

---

sive sanctification is "the work of God's free grace [2 Thess 2:13] whereby we are renewed in the whole man after the image of God [Eph 4:23–24], and are enabled more and more to die unto sin, and live unto righteousness [Rom 6:4, 6; 8:1]."
4. David Martyn Lloyd-Jones, "'Living the Christian Life'—New Developments in the 18th and 19th-Century Teaching," in *The Puritans: Their Origins and Successors;*

But the New Testament teaches that from the moment of justification, progressive sanctification is experientially actual (not merely potential or possible) for all Christians. It is impossible for a Christian to be justified without at the same time experiencing progressive sanctification. That theme features prominently in Romans 5-8.[5]

The primary issue Romans 1:18-11:36 addresses is righteousness. God is righteous in that he always acts in accordance with what is right. "The righteousness of God" is what God *is* when he saves you and what he *gives* you when he saves you. It is "his unswerving commitment to preserve the honor of his name and display his glory."[6]

- We are all sinners who need God's righteousness because God has condemned us (1:18-3:20).
- We can obtain God's righteousness by faith alone (3:21-4:25).
- We experience glorious results when we obtain God's righteousness (chaps. 5-8):
  - God reconciles us to himself (chap. 5).
  - God frees us from the dominating power of sin (chap. 6).
  - God frees us from the law (chap. 7).
  - God gives us security or assurance under the reign of grace (chap. 8).

Romans 6 is the key chapter in the Bible on progressive sanctification. Figure 3.4 traces the argument in Romans 6 by phrasing it.[7] It codes some recurring concepts, especially sin (underlined), slavery/freedom (caps), death (small caps), and life (bold). You don't need to understand all the

---

Addresses Delivered at the Puritan and Westminster Conferences, 1959-1978 (Carlisle, PA: Banner of Truth Trust, 1987), 322.

5. See Jonathan R. Pratt, "The Relationship between Justification and Spiritual Fruit in Romans 5-8," *Themelios* 34 (2009): 162-78. Pratt convincingly proves his thesis: "Romans 5-8 demonstrates that an obedient lifestyle inevitably and necessarily flows from justification" (164).

6. John Piper, *The Justification of God: An Exegetical and Theological Study of Romans 9:1-23*, in vol. 1 of *The Collected Works of John Piper*, ed. David Mathis and Justin Taylor (Wheaton, IL: Crossway, 2017), 413.

7. For an introduction to argument diagrams with a focus on phrasing, see Andrew David Naselli, *How to Understand and Apply the New Testament: Twelve Steps from Exegesis to Theology* (Phillipsburg, NJ: P&R Publishing, 2017), 121-61. I prepared the phrase diagrams in this book using www.biblearc.com.

nuances of phrasing to get the gist of figure 3.4: the resounding theme of Romans 6 is that all Christians without exception inevitably "walk in newness of life" (Rom 6:4).[8] Everyone is a slave—either a slave to sin or a slave to God and righteousness. If you are a Christian, then you serve a new master; sin is no longer your master.

"The whole point of Romans 6" is that "God not only frees us from sin's penalty (justification), but He frees us from sin's tyranny as well (sanctification)."[9] "A major flaw" with how higher life theology interprets Romans 6 is that "Paul is not telling believers *how* a justified person can lead a holy life, but *why he must* lead a holy life."[10]

---

8. Cf. John Murray, *The Epistle to the Romans: The English Text with Introduction, Exposition and Notes*, 2 vols., NICNT (Grand Rapids: Eerdmans, 1959-1965), 1:211-38; Douglas J. Moo, *The Epistle to the Romans*, NICNT (Grand Rapids: Eerdmans, 1996), 350-408; Thomas R. Schreiner, *Romans*, BECNT (Grand Rapids: Baker Academic, 1998), 298-342; MacArthur, *Faith Works: The Gospel according to the Apostles* (Dallas: Word, 1993), 105-21; Sinclair B. Ferguson, "The Reformed View," in *Christian Spirituality: Five Views of Sanctification*, ed. Donald Alexander (Downers Grove, IL: InterVarsity Press, 1988), 52-60; Peterson, *Possessed by God*, 96-103; Murray J. Harris, *Slave of Christ: A New Testament Metaphor for Total Devotion to Christ*, New Studies in Biblical Theology 8 (Downers Grove, IL: InterVarsity Press, 1999), 80-85; William W. Combs, "The Disjunction between Justification and Sanctification in Contemporary Evangelical Theology," *Detroit Baptist Seminary Journal* 6 (2001): 33-37.
9. MacArthur, *Faith Works*, 121. Cf. Benjamin B. Warfield, "The Victorious Life," in *Perfectionism: Volume II*, vol. 8 of *The Works of Benjamin B. Warfield* (New York: Oxford University Press, 1932), 568-69: "The whole sixth chapter of Romans ... was written for no other purpose than to assert and demonstrate that justification and sanctification are indissolubly bound together; that we cannot have the one without having the other; that, to use its own figurative language, dying with Christ and living with Christ are integral elements in one indisintegrable salvation. To wrest these two things apart and make separable gifts of grace of them evinces a confusion in the conception of Christ's salvation which is nothing less than portentous."
10. Combs, "Disjunction," 34. Cf. J. I. Packer, *Keep in Step with the Spirit: Finding Fullness in Our Walk with God*, 2nd ed. (Grand Rapids: Baker Books, 2005), 130-31.

Fig. 3.4. Phrase Diagram of Romans 6:1–23

6:1	What shall we say then?	
b	Are we to continue in sin	Wrong inference of 5:20–21
c	that grace may abound?	
6:2	By no means!	Answer to 1
b	How can we who died to sin still live in it?	Reason for 2a
6:3	Do you not know that all of us who have been baptized into Christ Jesus were baptized into his DEATH?	Explains 2b
6:4	We were buried therefore with him by baptism into DEATH,	Inference of 3; 4b–c = purpose of 4a
b	in order that, just as Christ was **raised** from the DEAD by the glory of the Father,	
c	we too might walk in **newness of life.**	
6:5	For if we have been united with him in a DEATH like his,	Supports 4
b	we shall certainly be united with him in a **resurrection** like his.	
6:6	We know that our old self was CRUCIFIED with him	Supports 5
b	in order that the body of sin might be BROUGHT TO NOTHING,	Purpose of 6a
c	so that we would no longer be ENSLAVED TO sin.	Result of 6a–b
6:7	For one who has DIED has been SET FREE FROM sin.	Supports 6
6:8	Now if we have DIED with Christ,	Develops 7; resumes 5
b	we believe that we will also **live** with him.	
6:9	We know that Christ, being **raised** from the dead, will never DIE again;	Supports 8
b	DEATH no longer HAS DOMINION OVER him.	
6:10	For the DEATH he DIED he DIED to sin, once for all,	Supports 9
b	but the **life** he **lives** he **lives** to God.	
6:11	So you also must consider yourselves DEAD to sin	Inference of 1–10
b	and **alive** to God	
c	in Christ Jesus.	
6:12	Let not sin therefore REIGN in your mortal body,	Inference of 1–11
b	to MAKE YOU OBEY its passions.	Result of 12a
6:13	Do not present your members to sin as instruments for unrighteousness,	Explains 12
b	but present yourselves to God as those who have been brought from DEATH to **life,**	Contrast to 13a
c	and your members to God as instruments for **righteousness**.	
6:14	For sin will HAVE NO DOMINION OVER you,	Supports 12–13
b	since you are not under LAW	Reason for 14a
c	but under **grace.**	
6:15	What then?	
b	Are we to sin	Wrong inference of 14b–c
c	because we are not under LAW	
d	but under **grace?**	
e	By no means!	Answers 15a–d
6:16	Do you not know that	
b	if you present yourselves to anyone as OBEDIENT SLAVES,	
c	you ARE SLAVES OF THE ONE WHOM YOU OBEY,	Reason for 15e
d	either of sin, which leads to DEATH,	
e	or of OBEDIENCE, which leads to **righteousness?**	

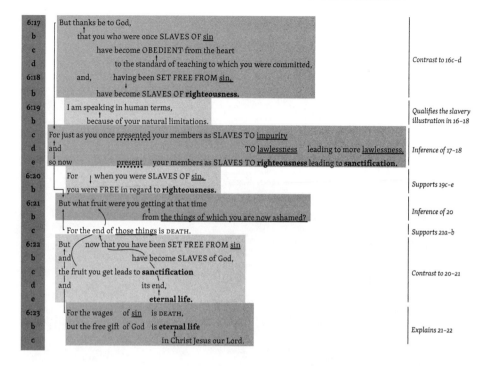

6:17	But thanks be to God,	
b	that you who were once SLAVES OF sin	
c	have become OBEDIENT from the heart	
d	to the standard of teaching to which you were committed,	Contrast to 16c–d
6:18	and, having been SET FREE FROM sin,	
b	have become SLAVES OF **righteousness.**	
6:19	I am speaking in human terms,	Qualifies the slavery
b	because of your natural limitations.	illustration in 16–18
c	For just as you once presented your members as SLAVES TO impurity	
d	and TO lawlessness leading to more lawlessness,	Inference of 17–18
e	so now present your members as SLAVES TO **righteousness** leading to **sanctification.**	
6:20	For when you were SLAVES OF sin,	Supports 19c–e
b	you were FREE in regard to **righteousness.**	
6:21	But what fruit were you getting at that time	Inference of 20
b	from the things of which you are now ashamed?	
c	For the end of those things is DEATH.	Supports 21a–b
6:22	But now that you have been SET FREE FROM sin	
b	and have become SLAVES of God,	
c	the fruit you get leads to **sanctification**	Contrast to 20–21
d	and its end,	
e	**eternal life.**	
6:23	For the wages of sin is DEATH,	
b	but the free gift of God is **eternal life**	Explains 21–22
c	in Christ Jesus our Lord.	

2. ALL CHRISTIANS ARE SPIRITUAL; NONE ARE PERMANENTLY CARNAL (1 CORINTHIANS 2:6–3:4)

The key text in this spiritual-versus-carnal debate is 1 Corinthians 2:6–3:4, and figure 3.5 lays out that passage by phrasing it. Again, you don't need to understand all the nuances of phrasing to see the debated issue: Paul describes people as natural, spiritual, and carnal (or "of the flesh"). The issue is whether those are three distinct categories.

Fig. 3.5. Phrase Diagram of 1 Corinthians 2:6–3:4

2:6	Yet among the mature we do **impart** WISDOM,	Contrast to 4–5
b	although it is not a WISDOM of this age	Concessive to 6a
c	or of the rulers of this age,	
d	who are doomed to pass away.	Describes 6c
2:7	But we **impart** a secret and hidden WISDOM of God,	Contrast to 6b–d
b	WHICH God decreed	Describes 7a
c	before the ages	Time of 7b
d	for our glory.	Purpose of 7b
2:8	None of the rulers of this age **understood** THIS,	Describes 7a
b	for if they had,	Condition of 8c
c	they would not have crucified the Lord of glory.	Supports 8a
2:9	But, as it is written,	Contrast to 8a (goes with 10a)
b	"What no eye has **seen**	
c	nor ear **heard**,	Content of 10a (i.e., what God has revealed)
d	nor the heart of man **imagined**,	
e	what God has prepared for those who love him"—	
2:10	these things God has revealed to us through the Spirit.	Continues 9a
b	For the Spirit searches everything,	Supports 10a
c	even the **depths** of God.	Describes 10b
2:11	For who **knows** a person's **thoughts**	
b	except the spirit of that person,	Supports 10b–c
c	which is in him?	
d	So also no one **comprehends** the **thoughts** of God	Supports 10b–c, compares to 11a–c
e	except the Spirit of God.	
2:12	Now we have **received** not the spirit of the world,	Explains the Spirit in 10–11
b	but the Spirit who is from God,	Contrast to 12a
c	that we might **understand** the things freely given us by God.	Purpose of 12a–b
2:13	And we **impart** this in words not taught by human WISDOM	Explains imparting in 6a, 7a
b	but taught by the Spirit,	Contrast to 13a
c	**interpreting** spiritual truths to those who are spiritual.	Means of 13a–b
2:14	The natural person does not **accept** the things of the Spirit of God,	Contrast to 13c
b	for they are folly to him,	Reason for 14a
c	and he is not able to **understand** them	Continues 14a
d	because they are spiritually **discerned**.	Reason for 14c
2:15	The spiritual person **judges** all things,	Contrast to 14
b	but is himself to be **judged** by no one.	Contrast to 15a
2:16	"For who has **understood** the **mind** of the Lord	Supports 14–15
b	so as to **instruct** him?"	
c	But we have the **mind** of Christ.	Qualifies 16a–b
3:1	But I, brothers,[e] could not address you	Contrast to the spiritual in 2:13–16
b	as spiritual people,	
c	but as people of the flesh,	Contrast to 1b
d	as infants in Christ.	
3:2	I fed you with milk,	Inference of 1
b	not solid food,	Contrast to 2a
c	for you were not ready for it.	Reason for 2a–b
d	And even now you are not yet ready,	Intensifies rebuke in 3c
3:3	for you are still of the flesh.	Reason for 2d
b	For while there is jealousy and strife among you,	
c	are you not of the flesh	Supports 3a
d	and behaving only in a human way?	
3:4	For when one says, "I follow Paul,"	
b	and another, "I follow Apollos,"	Supports 3
c	are you not being merely human?	

Figure 3.6 shows how nine translations render key words in 1 Corinthians 2:14–3:3:

Fig. 3.6. Translations of Key Words in 1 Corinthians 2:14–15; 3:1, 3

Trans-lation	2:14 ψυχικὸς ἄνθρωπος, psychikos anthrōpos	2:15 πνευματικός, pneumatikos	3:1 σαρκίνοις, sarkinois	3:3a σαρκικοί, sarkikoi	3:3b κατὰ ἄνθρωπον περιπατεῖτε, kata anthrōpon peripateite
ESV	the natural person	the spiritual person	people of the flesh	of the flesh	behaving only in a human way
KJV	the natural man	he that is spiritual	carnal	carnal	walk as men
NKVJ	the natural man	he who is spiritual	carnal	carnal	behaving like *mere* men
NASB	a natural man	he who is spiritual	men of flesh	fleshly	walking like mere men
NIV	the person without the Spirit	the person with the Spirit	people who are still worldly	worldly	acting like mere humans
NET	the unbeliever	the one who is spiritual	people of the flesh	influenced by the flesh	behaving like unregenerate people
CSB	the person without the Spirit	the spiritual person	people of the flesh	worldly	behaving like mere humans
NLT	people who aren't spiritual	those who are spiritual	though you belonged to this world	controlled by your sinful nature	living like people of the world
CEB	people who are unspiritual	spiritual people	unspiritual people	unspiritual	living by human standards

In 1 Corinthians 2:14–15, Paul describes people as either "natural" (ψυχι-κός, *psychikos*) or "spiritual" (πνευματικός, *pneumatikos*). Those who are "natural" are the opposite of "spiritual" because they do not have the Spirit (cf. Jude 19). Those who are "spiritual" have the Spirit. The NIV translates those terms most clearly: "the person without the Spirit" and "the person with the Spirit." Thus, all humans are in one of two categories (see fig. 3.7):

Fig. 3.7. Two Categories in Which All Humans Fit

Category 1	Category 2
Non-Christian	Christian
Unregenerate	Regenerate
Unbelieving	Believing
Unrepentant	Repentant
Unconverted	Converted
Natural	Spiritual

Paul then rebukes the Corinthian believers for not acting like who they are (3:1–4). He addresses the Corinthians as "people of the flesh" (3:1) or "carnal" (KJV, NKJV). The question is whether "spiritual" and "carnal" are two distinct, exclusive categories into which believers fit. Based on the way the Corinthians were acting, Paul could not address them as who they actually were. Although they were people who had the Spirit, they were acting "as" (ὡς, *hōs*) or "like" people not having the Spirit because people having the Spirit characteristically live a certain way. That is why Paul addresses them this way. He is not laying out three categories into which all people fall: natural, carnal, and spiritual. Nor is Paul using *pneumatikos* in two separate ways—to all Christians in 2:15 but to only mature Christians in 3:1.

> His concern is singular: not to suggest classes of Christians or grades of spirituality, but to get the Corinthians to stop *thinking* [and behaving] like the people of this present age ....
> To suggest *two* meanings for πνευματικός [*pneumatikos*] ...

misses Paul's point. ... His ultimate point is: "Stop it! People of the Spirit simply must stop behaving the way you are."[11]

"Natural" people characteristically act in a "carnal" or "fleshly" way. The reverse is true as well: those who live in a characteristically fleshly way are unbelievers. Believers may *temporarily* live in a fleshly way, but believers by definition live in a characteristically righteous way. D. A. Carson explains that by calling the Corinthians *carnal*,

> Paul does not have in mind someone who has made a profession of faith, carried on in the Christian way for a short while, and then reverted to a lifestyle indistinguishable in every respect from that of the world. ... Of course, if professing Christians slip far enough, some further category has to be found for them. Paul has one. ... "Examine yourselves to see whether you are in the faith; test yourselves. Do you not realize that Christ Jesus is in you—unless, of course, you fail the test?" (2 Cor 13:5). In other words, if their drift away from the gospel becomes serious enough, Paul questions whether they are Christians at all. ... What this means is that it will not do to apply "carnal Christian" or "worldly Christian" to every person who has made a profession of faith, perhaps years ago, but who for umpteen years has lived without any evidence of Christian faith, life, repentance, values, or interest.

---

11. Gordon D. Fee, *The First Epistle to the Corinthians*, 2nd ed., NICNT (Grand Rapids: Eerdmans, 2014), 131. Cf. Gordon D. Fee, *God's Empowering Presence: The Holy Spirit in the Letters of Paul* (Peabody, MA: Hendrickson, 1994), 28-32, 93-112; D. A. Carson, *The Cross and Christian Ministry: An Exposition of Passages from 1 Corinthians* (Grand Rapids: Baker Books, 1993), 58-59, 62, 68-75; D. A. Carson and John D. Woodbridge, *Letters Along the Way: A Novel of the Christian Life* (Wheaton, IL: Crossway, 1993), 26-31; Combs, "Disjunction," 38-42; Mark A. Snoeberger, "The Logical Priority of Regeneration to Saving Faith in a Theological Ordo Salutis," *Detroit Baptist Seminary Journal* 7 (2002): 84-88; MacArthur, *Faith Works*, 124-27; Ernest C. Reisinger, *What Should We Think of "The Carnal Christian"?* (Carlisle, PA: Banner of Truth Trust, 1978), 6-12; David L. Eby, "The Reformed Response to the Higher Life Movement" (ThM thesis, Westminster Theological Seminary, 1982), 91-99; Kenneth S. Kantzer, "A Reformed View of Sanctification," in *Free and Fulfilled: Victorious Living in the 21st Century*, ed. Robertson McQuilkin (Nashville: Nelson, 1997), 216-17; Brian Borgman, "Rethinking a Much Abused Text: 1 Corinthians 3:1-15," *Reformation and Revival* 11, no. 1 (2002): 71-94.

In such instances it is far more likely than not that we are dealing with spurious conversions.[12]

Christians who are "carnal" (σάρκινος [sarkinos] and σαρκικός [sarkikos] in 1 Cor 3:1, 3) are only *temporarily* carnal—not permanently carnal. "The carnal Christian is simply a genuine Christian (Spirit-man) temporarily gone astray."[13]

Furthermore, the carnality does not necessarily extend equally to every area of a Christian's life, nor does it characterize a Christian's entire life-style. In the case of the Corinthians, Paul calls them fleshly specifically because they were being sinfully divisive. In this sense, one could say that all Christians prior to their glorification are fleshly to some degree in some areas but not characteristically so overall.[14] What this passage does *not* support is a permanent category called "carnal Christians" in which fruitless, fleshly professing believers may remain throughout their entire "Christian" life (see fig. 3.8).

Fig. 3.8. The Reformed View of Progressive Sanctification

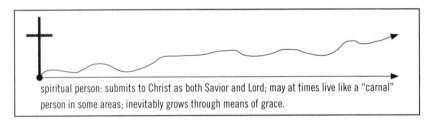

spiritual person: submits to Christ as both Savior and Lord; may at times live like a "carnal" person in some areas; inevitably grows through means of grace.

---

12. Carson, *The Cross and Christian Ministry*, 74.

13. Combs, "Disjunction," 41.

14. Bruce Demarest, *The Cross and Salvation: The Doctrine of Salvation*, Foundations of Evangelical Theology (Wheaton, IL: Crossway, 1997), 416: "No sharp dividing line exists to separate an alleged 'carnal Christian' from a 'spiritual Christian.' ... Every Christian is characterized by a measure of holiness and truth on one hand, and by a dose of carnality and worldliness on the other. The Christian is a pilgrim who progresses along the spectrum toward holiness and maturity in Christ. The believer does not arise one morning as a 'carnal Christian' and settle in that night as a 'spiritual Christian.' ... The terms 'spiritual' and 'carnal' apply to every Christian, although not in equal measure or in the same respects. Each of us struggles with carnality in different ways and with varying intensity as we press toward the goal of our high calling in Christ."

3. ALL CHRISTIANS ARE SPIRIT-BAPTIZED
(1 CORINTHIANS 12:13)

The New Testament mentions Spirit-baptism eleven times:

- John the Baptist predicts that it would occur (Matt 3:11; Mark 1:8; Luke 3:16; John 1:33).
- Jesus guarantees that it would occur (Acts 1:5; cf. Luke 11:13; 24:49; John 7:37–39; 14–17).
- Peter affirms that it did occur (Acts 11:16).
- Paul explains its theological significance (Rom 6:1–4; 1 Cor 12:13; Gal 3:27; Eph 4:5; Col 2:12).[15]

Spirit-baptism is Christ's judicially placing Christians in the Holy Spirit when God regenerates them, thus placing them into the body of Christ.[16] The central text for Spirit-baptism is 1 Corinthians 12:13: "For in one Spirit we were *all* baptized into one body—Jews or Greeks, slaves or free—and *all* were made to drink of one Spirit" (1 Cor 12:13, emphasis added). All Christians are Spirit-baptized. All Christians share "one baptism" (Eph 4:5). The New Testament never commands or exhorts Christians to pursue or receive Spirit-baptism because they are already Spirit-baptized.[17]

---

15. Scholars debate whether Paul refers to Spirit-baptism or water-baptism.

16. Scholars debate whether Christ performs Spirit-baptism *in the sphere* or *by the agency* of the Holy Spirit. The preposition ἐν (*en*) allows both interpretations because it can communicate either sphere (*in*) or personal agency (*by*). Personal agency is a respectable, orthodox view, but sphere seems more likely for grammatical and theological reasons. *Grammatically*, the first four references to Spirit-baptism all state that Christ is the one who baptizes in (ἐν, *en*) the Spirit, which parallels John the Baptist's baptizing in (ἐν, *en*) water (Matt 3:11; Mark 1:8; Luke 3:16; John 1:33). Just as John was the baptizer and the water was the element in which he baptized people, so Christ is the baptizer and the Spirit is the element or sphere in which Christ baptizes believers. Acts 1:5 and 11:16 maintain this same parallelism. The only text in which Paul uses the preposition *en* (ἐν) with reference to Spirit-baptism is 1 Corinthians 12:13: "For in [ἐν, *en*] one Spirit we were all baptized into [εἰς, *eis*] one body." *Theologically*, Christ is the baptizer because Peter declares in Acts 2:33 that Christ "has poured out this that you yourselves are seeing and hearing." Christ sent the Spirit at Pentecost, and Christ is the one who baptizes believers.

17. A minority of Reformed exegetes argue that there are two types of Spirit-baptism—the type I describe above and another type that Christians can experience later in their Christian life. E.g., see David Martyn Lloyd-Jones, *Great Doctrines of the Bible, Volume 2: God the Holy Spirit* (Wheaton, IL: Crossway, 1997), 234–40. The issue

While some advocates of higher life theology distinguish between Christians who are not Spirit-baptized (category 1) and those who are (category 2), most have conceded that all Christians are Spirit-baptized. But all advocates of higher life theology argue that not all Christians are Spirit-filled.

4. ALL CHRISTIANS ARE SPIRIT-FILLED TO VARIOUS DEGREES (EPHESIANS 5:18)

Ephesians 5:18 commands, "Be filled with the Spirit" (πληροῦσθε ἐν πνεύματι, *plērousthe en pneumati*). That is the only time Spirit-filling appears in Paul's letters, which suggests that higher life theology is out of balance when it makes Spirit-filling the secret key to victorious Christian living.[18] Before higher life theology in the 1800s, Christians did not emphasize Spirit-filling as the key to victorious Christian living.[19] That does not mean that Spirit-filling is unimportant. But the way higher life theology has focused on Spirit-filling is unwarranted. I'll demonstrate that by answering six questions:

1. What does "be filled" mean?
2. What does "with the Spirit" mean?
3. What are the results of Spirit-filling?
4. How do you obey the command "be filled with the Spirit"?
5. Are all Christians Spirit-filled?
6. Doesn't a command imply that you either obey it or disobey it?

---

depends largely on how you interpret stories in Acts where people who have already converted then experience Spirt-baptism. In those stories I think Acts describes what happened in a unique, transitional period of redemptive history. Cf. Gordon D. Fee and Douglas Stuart, *How to Read the Bible for All Its Worth*, 4th ed. (Grand Rapids: Zondervan, 2014), 124 (emphasis in original): "*Unless Scripture explicitly tells us we must do something, what is only narrated or described does not function in a normative (i.e. obligatory) way—unless it can be demonstrated on other grounds that the author intended it to function in this way.*"

18. Cf. Andreas J. Köstenberger, "What Does It Mean to Be Filled with the Spirit? A Biblical Investigation," *Journal of the Evangelical Theological Society* 40 (1997): 231.

19. Cf. William W. Combs, "Spirit-Filling in Ephesians 5:18," *Detroit Baptist Seminary Journal* 19 (2014): 25-31.

What Does "Be Filled" Mean?

The first half of Ephesians 5:18 helps you understand the second half: "And do not get drunk with wine, for that is debauchery, but be filled with the Spirit." Alcohol strongly influences a drunk person. A person who is normally timid and soft-spoken may become bold and outspoken when under the influence of alcohol. "Debauchery" characterizes a drunk person. "Be filled" is parallel to "do not get drunk." Just as alcohol *strongly influences* a drunk person, so the Spirit must *strongly influence* a Christian. That is the point of the analogy.[20]

It is common to define "be filled" as "be controlled." I think that is too strong because some may misunderstand "control" to mean absolute or total control in the sense that the Christian is completely passive (i.e., "*let go* and let God"). It is more precise to explain "be filled" as "be strongly influenced" because there are degrees of drunkenness. If the Spirit "totally controls" a Christian, then that implies the Christian will be completely sinless.[21]

"Be filled" translates πληροῦσθε (*plērousthe*), which is in the present tense-form; in context, this communicates that Christians should make this their ongoing habit or custom.[22] That verb is also passive, which means that the Christian is not the person who does the influencing. But that

---

20. R. Kent Hughes, *Ephesians: The Mystery of the Body of Christ*, Preaching the Word (Wheaton, IL: Crossway, 1990), 173: "It is true that when someone is drunk he is 'under the influence,' and when one is filled with the Spirit he is under the Spirit's influence. But the comparison ends here, and the rest is contrast. Being filled with the Spirit is not a kind of spiritual intoxication in which we lose self-control, for 'self-control' is a fruit of the Spirit (Galatians 5:22, 23; 2 Timothy 1:7). ... Those filled with the Spirit are not drunk with the Spirit! In addition to this, we must understand that alcohol is a *depressant*, while the Spirit is a *stimulant*."

21. Larry D. Pettegrew, *The New Covenant Ministry of the Holy Spirit*, 2nd ed. (Grand Rapids: Kregel, 2001), 204: "The word *control*, although often used as the meaning of filling, might be too strong. *Control* often has the connotation in our culture of something like total control over a puppet. It suggests either all or nothing. But this connotation is more than the metaphor implies. Wine does not control a person as though he were a puppet or a robot. Neither does the Holy Spirit. Just as there are increasing degrees of influence of wine on a person, so there should be increasing degrees of the influence of the Holy Spirit in the life of a Christian."

22. Cf. Daniel B. Wallace, *Greek Grammar beyond the Basics: An Exegetical Syntax of the New Testament* (Grand Rapids: Zondervan, 1996), 722, 521–22.

does not mean that you should passively wait for Spirit-filling to happen. God addresses this command to you, so you are responsible to obey it. Just as you are responsible not to let alcohol strongly influence you, so you are responsible to be filled with the Spirit.

What Does "with the Spirit" Mean?

Assuming that Paul refers to the Holy Spirit rather than a human spirit, the main issue is whether "with the Spirit" (ἐν πνεύματι, *en pneumati*) indicates *content* or *means* (see fig. 3.9).

Fig. 3.9. Illustrations of Content vs. Means

Content	Means
Fill a pool with water.	Fill a pool with a hose.
Fill a tire with air.	Fill a tire with an air-compressor.
Fill your stomach with food and drink.	Fill your stomach with forks and cups.
Fill a tooth's cavity with amalgam or composite.	Fill a tooth's cavity with dental tools.
Be filled with the Spirit.	Be filled by the Spirit.

Most interpreters—whether proponents of higher life theology or not—assume that *en pneumati* means "with the Spirit" (i.e., content), not "by the Spirit" (i.e., means). If Paul intends means and not content, then other passages in Ephesians that use the verb *fill* may indicate who does the filling (i.e., Christ—Eph 1:22; 4:10) and what the content is (i.e., "the fullness of God" or God's moral excellence—Eph 3:19). Thus, Wallace concludes, "Believers are to be filled *by* Christ *by means of* the Spirit *with* the content of the fullness of God."[23]

I used to be more confident that Paul intends to communicate means and not content,[24] but now I'm not as sure because you can make a good

---

23. Ibid., 375.

24. Andrew David Naselli, *Let Go and Let God? A Survey and Analysis of Keswick Theology* (Bellingham, WA: Lexham Press, 2010), 251–55. Cf. Wallace, *Greek Grammar beyond the Basics*, 375; Harold W. Hoehner, *Ephesians: An Exegetical Commentary* (Grand Rapids: Baker Academic, 2002), 703–4.

case for content.[25] I wonder if it may be both—parallel to how wine is both the content and means of getting drunk: "And do not get drunk with wine … but be filled with the Spirit."

WHAT ARE RESULTS OF SPIRIT-FILLING?

You can know you are Spirit-filled by comparing your life with the five result-participles in Ephesians 5:19–21: "*addressing* one another in psalms and hymns and spiritual songs, *singing* and *making melody* to the Lord with your heart, *giving thanks* always and for everything to God the Father in the name of our Lord Jesus Christ, *submitting* to one another out of reverence for Christ."[26] The degree to which those results are evident in your life is the degree to which the Spirit is influencing you.

HOW DO YOU OBEY THE COMMAND "BE FILLED WITH THE SPIRIT"?

Can you do something to increase the level to which the Spirit influences you? The most helpful passage in this regard is Colossians 3:16–4:1, the parallel passage to Ephesians 5:18–6:9. In Colossians 3:16–17, Paul lists results that are virtually identical to those in Ephesians 5:19–20. But in Colossians 3:16, the initial command before the result participles is different: "Let the word of Christ dwell in you richly." That is parallel to the command "Be filled with the Spirit."[27] So letting the word of Christ dwell in you richly is a way to let the Spirit strongly influence you. That is a lifelong process.

---

25. Cf. Clinton E. Arnold, *Ephesians*, Zondervan Exegetical Commentary on the New Testament (Grand Rapids: Zondervan, 2010), 349–51; Combs, "Spirit-Filling in Ephesians 5:18," 36–40.

26. In 5:22–6:9, Paul develops the result of submitting to one another in three household relationships: husbands and wives, parents and children, and masters and slaves.

27. Robert L. Reymond, *A New Systematic Theology of the Christian Faith*, 2nd ed. (Nashville: Nelson, 1998), 766: "These two ideas, both highlighting a divine, *subjective* influence, are practically identical. To be filled with the Spirit is to be indwelt by the word of Christ; to be indwelt by the word of Christ is to be filled with the Spirit. One must never separate the Spirit from Christ's word or Christ's word from the Spirit. The Spirit works by and with Christ's word. Christ's word works by and with the Spirit."

Are All Christians Spirit-Filled?

Higher life theology says *No,* but so do some who oppose higher life theology.[28] Both assume that Christians are either completely filled or empty. It seems more accurate to say that the Spirit is influencing every believer *to some degree*—some more strongly than others. It is not all or nothing. The issue is not whether a Christian has all of the Spirit because a Christian is by definition someone who has the Spirit (e.g., 1 Cor 2:14–15). The issue is whether the Spirit has all of the Christian.

Being Spirit-filled is not like turning on a light by flipping a toggle switch. It is like a dimmer switch that is always on; sometimes the light is bright, and sometimes it is not so bright. Spirit-filling is not a mystical experience limited to an elite group of Christians who have experienced a crisis of consecration.[29] Spirit-filling occurs in all Christians to some degree—just like Christians bear fruit to different degrees (see Matt 13:23).

Doesn't a Command Imply That You Either Obey It or Disobey It?

Not necessarily. Not all commands are as simple as ones I might give to my little children: "Sit down." "Get in the van." "Go to your room." "Throw the ball." Those commands are straightforward. The child either obeys or disobeys. It's like a toggle switch—the light is either on or off. There's no dimmer.

Higher life theology rejects the possibility that all Christians are filled with the Spirit to various degrees because it assumes that the command "Be filled with the Spirit" indicates that Christians either completely obey it or completely disobey it.

In the New Testament there are over 1,400 commands directed to "you" (i.e., second-person imperatives). Most of them appeal to your will and assume that you can obey the command. And most have a black-and-white nature; you either completely obey them or don't. But some commands that

---

28. John MacArthur, *Charismatic Chaos* (Grand Rapids: Zondervan, 1992), 314–15: "You can be filled today, but tomorrow is another story. ... Obviously, a lot of believers are *not* filled with the Spirit."

29. Thomas Edgar, "The Sufficiency of Our Justification," *Conservative Theological Journal* 2 (1998): 234: Being filled by the Spirit is not "an event obtainable by 'full surrender' ... any more than the admonition 'to be filled with knowledge' means that there is an event obtainable by 'full surrender' such as 'the filling with knowledge.'"

the New Testament addresses to Christians are not all-or-nothing. Obeying and disobeying these commands are not always like flipping a toggle switch but may be more like moving a dimmer switch. Here are some commands that you can obey to various degrees:

- "make disciples of all nations" (Matt 28:19)
- "Do not be conformed to this world, but be transformed by the renewal of your mind" (Rom 12:2)
- "glorify God in your body" (1 Cor 6:20)
- "do all to the glory of God" (1 Cor 10:31)
- "do not go on sinning" (1 Cor 15:34)
- "through love serve one another" (Gal 5:13)
- "walk by the Spirit" (Gal 5:16)
- "Be kind to one another" (Eph 4:32)
- "be imitators of God" (Eph 5:1)
- "walk in love" (Eph 5:2)
- "Walk as children of light" (Eph 5:8)
- "Look carefully then how you walk" (Eph 5:15)
- "do not be foolish, but understand what the will of the Lord is" (Eph 5:17)
- "be filled with the Spirit" (Eph 5:18)
- "Husbands, love your wives" (Eph 5:25)
- "be strong in the Lord and in the strength of his might" (Eph 6:10)
- "Have this mind among yourselves, which is yours in Christ Jesus" (Phil 2:5)
- "rejoice in the Lord" (Phil 3:1)
- "Rejoice in the Lord always; again I will say, rejoice" (Phil 4:4)
- "encourage one another and build one another up, just as you are doing" (1 Thess 5:11)
- "Rejoice always, pray without ceasing, give thanks in all circumstances" (1 Thess 5:16–18)
- "Fight the good fight of the faith" (1 Tim 6:12)
- "as he who called you is holy, you also be holy in all your conduct" (1 Pet 1:15)
- "love one another earnestly from a pure heart" (1 Pet 1:22)
- "Do not love the world or the things in the world" (1 John 2:15)

Here are six observations about those commands:

1. Christians obey some commands to various degrees. I love my wife, but I could love her to a greater degree (Eph 5:25).

2. Christians obey broad and all-encompassing commands (e.g., "glorify God") to various degrees *in various areas*.

3. The command "be filled with the Spirit" (Eph 5:18) occurs in the context of similar commands in Ephesians 4–6 (cf. Col 3:1–2, 18–19, 23; 4:2). That makes it even more likely that "be filled with the Spirit" is not an all-or-nothing command.

4. In 1 Thessalonians 5:11, Paul commands the Thessalonians to do what they are already doing. That further supports that Paul could command Christians to be filled with the Spirit when they are *already* filled with the Spirit.

5. Some commands are characteristically true of all believers to various degrees. For example, Galatians 5:16 ("walk by the Spirit")—all Christians characteristically keep in step with the Spirit to some degree because the only other option is to "gratify the desires of the flesh," and "those who do such things will not inherit the kingdom of God" (Gal 5:16, 21). Or 1 John 2:15 ("Do not love the world or the things in the world")—all Christians don't love the world to various degrees because the rest of the passage continues, "If anyone loves the world, the love of the Father is not in him."

6. These commands are God-ordained means to enable Christians to persevere—similar to passages like 1 Corinthians 9:24; Philippians 2:12; Hebrews 3:12–15; 12:14; and Jude 21.[30] God enables all genuine Christians to persevere, so all Christians will persevere. But Christians must never rationalize, "Since I am already a Christian, I am persevering by definition, so I do not need to be concerned about obeying those commands." God forbid! Such commands are God-ordained means of grace for Christians to continue persevering. Similarly, commands such as "Love one another" and "Be filled with the Spirit" are God-ordained means of grace for Christians to continue to mature. Such commands should convict Christians and spur them to obey to greater degrees by God's grace. Chris-

---

30. For more on perseverance, see reason 6 below.

tians must never rationalize, "Since I am already obeying this command to a certain degree, I do not need to be concerned about obeying it to a greater degree." God forbid!

Another command that you can obey to various degrees is in John 15:4: "Abide in me, and I in you."

5. ALL CHRISTIANS ABIDE IN CHRIST TO VARIOUS DEGREES (JOHN 15:1–10)

[1]I am the true vine, and my Father is the vinedresser. [2]Every branch in me that does not bear fruit he takes away, and every branch that does bear fruit he prunes, that it may bear more fruit. [3]Already you are clean because of the word that I have spoken to you. [4]Abide in me, and I in you. As the branch cannot bear fruit by itself, unless it abides in the vine, neither can you, unless you abide in me. [5]I am the vine; you are the branches. Whoever abides in me and I in him, he it is that bears much fruit, for apart from me you can do nothing. [6]If anyone does not abide in me he is thrown away like a branch and withers; and the branches are gathered, thrown into the fire, and burned. [7]If you abide in me, and my words abide in you, ask whatever you wish, and it will be done for you. [8]By this my Father is glorified, that you bear much fruit and so prove to be my disciples. [9]As the Father has loved me, so have I loved you. Abide in my love. [10]If you keep my commandments, you will abide in my love, just as I have kept my Father's commandments and abide in his love. (John 15:1–10)

The verb "abide" in verse 4 translates μένω (menō). The ESV, KJV, NKJV, and NASB all translate it as "abide." But *abide* can sound strangely mystical. Largely because higher life theology is so influential, many Christians desire to *become* Christians who abide—an experience they view as a deeper, more intimate resting in Jesus that is a second tier in the Christian life. Higher life theology assumes that only *some* believers abide: those who do not abide are carnal Christians, and those who abide are spiritual or Spirit-filled Christians.

But the New Testament teaches that *all* believers characteristically abide to some degree and that the concept is a metaphor for perseverance.[31] Μένω basically means to remain, which is why several modern translations render it as "remain" in John 15:4 (NIV, NET, CSB, NLT, CEB, NJB). Μένω never occurs in the New Testament in a way that supports a category of Christians who do not abide.[32]

John 15:1–10 is the main text for abiding, and there are three major views on the passage. The key issue is identifying the fruitless branch in verses 2 and 6.

1. The fruitless branch represents a genuine Christian who forfeits their salvation and then experiences eternal damnation.

2. The fruitless branch represents a carnal Christian whom the Father either tenderly nurtures or severely chastises.

3. The fruitless branch represents a professing Christian who evidences that their connection to Christ is superficial and then experiences eternal damnation.

Higher life theology holds the second view, and I think the third is correct. I'll walk through the passage to explain why.

WHAT DOES THE METAPHOR OF ABIDING MEAN (JOHN 15:1–6)?

A metaphor is an implied comparison without *like* or *as*. For example, "All flesh is grass" (Isa 40:6) or "Herod is a fox."

A metaphor has three parts: (1) the topic or item that the image illustrates; (2) the image; and (3) the point of similarity or comparison. Sometimes one or two of the three components may be implicit rather than explicit.

1. All flesh is grass.
    1. Topic: All flesh.
    2. Image: grass.
    3. Point of similarity: short-lived, perishable.

---

31. D. Kipp Johnson, "Johannine Abiding: Perseverance in the Faith" (ThM thesis, Dallas Theological Seminary, 1975); Sambhu Nath De, "The Meaning of 'Abiding' in the Johannine Writings" (ThD diss., Central Baptist Theological Seminary, 1991).
32. Naselli, *Let Go and Let God?*, 312–20 ("Appendix C: A Word Study on ΜΕΝΩ [Abide]").

2. Herod is a fox.
    1. Topic: Herod.
    2. Image: fox.
    3. Point of similarity: Four legs? Red? Furry? No, *sly*.

Warning: Talking about the point of similarity this way can be misleading. "Herod is a fox" and "Herod is sly" are not identical statements. You can't substitute "sly" for "fox" and maintain an equivalent meaning with all the same connotations. A metaphor communicates distinctively. But breaking down the components like this is a helpful way to analyze it.

Let's try doing this for an extended metaphor in John 15. (This part of the book sounds a little like a commentary, but stick with me because John 15 is a key passage for either supporting or refuting higher life theology. I attempt to show that John 15 *refutes* higher life theology.)

Analyzing this extended metaphor is more challenging than analyzing a simple statement like "Herod is a fox" because that simple statement explicitly names the topic and image. But the extended metaphor in John 15 includes several images without explicitly naming the topics. Figure 3.10 displays the topics that the images in Jesus' metaphor illustrate as well as the point of similarity between each topic and image.

Fig. 3.10. The Components of Jesus' Metaphor in John 15

1. Item	2. Image	3. Point of Similarity
a. Jesus	The true vine	The exclusive source of fruitfulness
b. God the Father	The vinedresser	Ensures increased fruitfulness
c. Those connected to Jesus: 1. Judas: counterfeit believer 2. eleven disciples: genuine believers	Branches: 1. fruitless branches 2. fruitful branches	Connection to the source of fruitfulness: 1. non-vital connection 2. vital connection
d. Jesus' words	Pruning knife (*implied*)	Means of cleansing to increase fruitfulness
e. What Christians produce	Fruit	Product of vital connection
f. How Christians produce it	Remaining vitally connected	Abiding

a. A vine pours life into its branches, and that is the only way its branches can be fruitful. In contrast to barren Israel (cf. Isa 5:1–7; Jer 2:21), Jesus is "the true vine" (John 15:1), the exclusive source of fruitfulness.

b. A vinedresser increases the fruitfulness of the vine by pruning it, that is, removing dead branches or stems and superfluous or undesired parts. Verse 2 contains a word play: αἴρει (*airei*, "he takes away, removes") and καθαίρει (*kathairei*, "he prunes").

c. Every unfruitful branch connected to the vine ("in me," v. 2) is removed, thrown away, dried up, gathered, cast into the fire, and burned (v. 6).[33] Unfruitful branches show that they are only superficially connected to the vine. As Jesus spoke these words to his

---

33. Edwin A. Blum, "John," in *The Bible Knowledge Commentary: An Exposition of the Scriptures*, ed. John F. Walvoord and Roy B. Zuck, 2 vols. (Wheaton, IL: Victor, 1983–1985), 2:325: "The phrase 'in Me' does not mean the same thing as Paul's words 'in Christ.' Here it is part of the metaphor of the Vine and seems to mean, 'every person who professes to be My disciple (a "branch") is not necessarily a true follower.'"

eleven disciples, Judas was showing that he was only superficially connected to Jesus:

> Now before the Feast of the Passover, when Jesus knew that his hour had come to depart out of this world to the Father, having loved his own who were in the world, he loved them to the end. During supper, when the devil had already put it into the heart of Judas Iscariot, Simon's son, to betray him .... Jesus said to him, "The one who has bathed does not need to wash, except for his feet, but is completely clean. And you are clean, but not every one of you." For he knew who was to betray him; that was why he said, "Not all of you are clean." (John 13:1–2, 10–11)

Judas betrayed Jesus. In contrast to Judas, the eleven disciples were fruitful and clean.[34] Judas represents spurious believers who are only superficially connected to Jesus, and the eleven disciples represent genuine believers who are vitally connected to Jesus.[35]

d. Verses 2 and 3 employ another word play: καθαίρει (kathairei, "he prunes") and καθαροί (katharoi, "clean"). A vinedresser prunes branches with a knife. He personally gives careful attention to each fruitful branch, and he cuts or snips off parts of fruitful branches so that they will bear more fruit. The Father's instrument for pruning the eleven disciples was Jesus' words.

e. Jesus refers to no fruit (vv. 2, 4), fruit (v. 2), more fruit (v. 2), and much fruit (vv. 5, 8). Fruit is what branches produce when they are vitally connected to the vine.

f. Branches that produce fruit show that they are vitally connected to the vine. Professing Christians who do not produce fruit (e.g., Judas) show that they are only superficially connected to Jesus, and Christians who produce fruit (e.g., the eleven disciples) show

---

34. Jesus tells the eleven disciples "Already you are clean" (John 15:3), excluding Judas, the unfruitful branch. Earlier that same evening, Jesus told the disciples, "You are clean, but not every one of you" (13:10), because he knew Judas would betray him (13:11).

35. See D. A. Carson, *The Gospel according to John*, Pillar New Testament Commentary (Grand Rapids: Eerdmans, 1991), 515.

that they are vitally connected to Jesus. Christians must abide in order to bear fruit.

What Does Jesus' Command to Abide Mean (John 15:4a)?

Μένω occurs ten times in verses 4–10 (v. 4 [3x], 5, 6, 7 [2x], 9, 10 [2x]), and Jesus implies it twice (vv. 4, 5). But Jesus does not initially define abiding; he commands it: "Abide in me, and I in you" (v. 4a). This command implies that believers are already vitally connected to Jesus and are responsible to maintain that vital connection. Such a command is a God-ordained means for believers to persevere.[36]

What Reasons Does Jesus Give for Abiding (John 15:4–6)?

Three reasons: (1) Fruitfulness is impossible apart from abiding in Jesus (vv. 4–5). (2) Abiding results in fruitfulness (v. 5). (3) Failing to abide results in final judgment (v. 6). The burned branch in verse 6 must refer to people who have professed to follow Jesus but who did not actually follow him. They appeared to be connected, but they were not actually connected.[37] "They went out from us, but they were not of us; for if they had been of us, they would have continued with us. But they went out, that it might become plain that they all are not of us" (1 John 2:19). All genuine believers are fruitful (cf. Matt 7:16–17; Rom 6; Eph 2:10; Jas 2:14–26).[38] The fruitless branches in John 15 do not represent non-Spirit-filled believers in contrast

---

36. Hoekema, *Saved by Grace*, 246; James E. Rosscup, *Abiding in Christ: Studies in John 15* (Grand Rapids: Zondervan, 1973), 146–70; Thomas R. Schreiner and Ardel B. Caneday, *The Race Set before Us: A Biblical Theology of Perseverance and Assurance* (Downers Grove, IL: InterVarsity Press, 2001), 38–45. For more on perseverance, see reason 6 on p. 88: "False Assurance."

37. Rosscup, *Abiding in Christ*, 211–37.

38. Ibid., 187: "Some cloud the issue by making it appear that if we say fruit is necessary in the Christian life, we are then subtly teaching a salvation by performance rather than by grace. Their emphasis is relevant against a works-salvation system, but it is a 'straw man' if used against the view taken in this chapter. It springs from misunderstanding or else misrepresentation of what the view actually is. Fruit is not simply nice; it is necessary. It does not merit salvation, but does manifest it once it really is there. It does not earn it, but does express it; it does not secure it, but is a sign of it; it is not a condition of conversion, but a consequence."

to Spirit-filled believers. Fruitless branches represent counterfeit professing believers whom God will finally judge as unbelievers.

HOW DOES JESUS EXPLAIN ABIDING (JOHN 15:7–10)?

1. Jesus explains what it means for him to abide in believers. The difference between verses 4 and 7 is significant: "Abide in me, and I in you" (v. 4) and "If you abide in me and *my words* abide in you" (v. 7, emphasis added). "My words" (v. 7) explains "I in you" (v. 4). (See fig. 3.11.) Jesus resides in believers when his specific utterances reside in believers (cf. 6:63). Jesus rebuked Philip in 14:10, "Do you not believe that I am in the Father and the Father is in me? The words that I say to you I do not speak on my own authority, but the Father who dwells [from μένω] in me does his works." The Father resides in Jesus in that his words reside in Jesus. We can't fully understand how the Father and Son relate to each other, but their relationship illustrates how Jesus resides in believers, namely, through his words (cf. 8:31).

2. Jesus explains the result of his abiding in believers: "ask whatever you wish, and it will be done for you. By this my Father is glorified, that you bear much fruit and so prove to be my disciples" (vv. 7b–8). When believers internalize Jesus' individual utterances, they will make scripturally informed requests, and God will answer them (cf. 14:13–14). The fruit in this context is the answers to those prayers (v. 8). Bearing much fruit in this way glorifies God the Father and shows that you are Jesus' disciple.

3. Jesus explains what it means for believers to abide in him. The difference between verses 4 and 9 is significant: "Abide in me" (v. 4) and "Abide in my love" (v. 9). The second command further specifies what "Abide in me" means, and verse 10 clarifies what it means to abide in Jesus' love: "If you keep my commandments, you will abide in my love." Jesus abides in believers when his words abide in them, and believers abide in Jesus when they obey his words. Abiding in Jesus is obeying Jesus: "Whoever keeps his com-

mandments abides in God, and God in him" (1 John 3:24).[39] Thus, "Abide in me, and I in you" (v. 4) means "Obey my words, and let my words remain in you." (See fig. 3.11.)

Fig. 3.11. Explaining John 15:4 with 15:7, 9–10

	"Abide in me" = Obey my words	"I in you" = Let my words remain in you
v. 4	"Abide in me"	"and I in you"
v. 7	"If you abide in me"	"and *my words* abide in you"
vv. 9–10	"Abide in my love. If you *keep my commandments*, you will abide in my love"	

Jesus abides in you to the degree that his words abide in you, and you abide in Jesus to the degree that you obey his words. Every believer abides in Jesus to some degree, and that results in different degrees of fruitfulness.[40]

---

39. The way John uses μένω (*menō*) in 1–2 John confirms that he does not distinguish between an abiding, Spirit-filled believer and a non-abiding, carnal believer. Such a view wrongly interprets μένω (*menō*) as an activity that only some believers do. See Naselli, *Let Go and Let God?*, 247–50.

40. Rosscup, *Abiding in Christ*, 171, 180 (cf. 106–26): "Every truly saved person, in the overall thrust of his life, does abide in Christ. By this it is meant that he continues in his new life in Christ. The difference between Christians is in the matter of the consistency, degree, depth, and richness of intimacy with the Lord. This relates to the *quality* aspect in abiding. ... The time you have been a Christian plus your knowledge of the Word (breadth, depth of insight) plus the degree or vital quality aspect of your abiding determines your level of growth and maturity."

CHAPTER 4

Nine More Reasons Higher Life Theology Is Harmful

The number one reason higher life theology is harmful is its disjunction—it creates two categories of Christians. That reason alone is a sufficient reason to reject it. Yet there are at least nine more reasons it is harmful (which we label as reasons 2–10 below).

REASON 2. A FORM OF PERFECTIONISM
It Portrays a Shallow and Incomplete
View of Sin in the Christian Life

Higher life theology does not advocate Christian perfection like Wesleyan perfectionism does, but it is still a form of perfectionism because its view of sin in the Christian life is shallow and incomplete.[1] The Welsh preacher Martyn Lloyd-Jones labeled higher life theology as "Psychological Perfectionism."[2]

---

1. J. I. Packer, *Keep in Step with the Spirit: Finding Fullness in Our Walk with God*, 2nd ed. (Grand Rapids: Baker Books, 2005), 126: "its architects were laymen and pastors whose agenda was to dissociate themselves from Wesleyan perfectionism while retaining the Wesleyan second-blessing frame, and it may be that the wider theological implications of the concepts they formed as means to this end escaped them. However, if we take their words at face value, the judgment expressed above is inescapable. They really did affirm a perfection of acts, and they really did deny that after conversion God further changes our hearts, and both claims are wrong."
2. David Martyn Lloyd-Jones, "'Living the Christian Life'—New Developments in the 18th and 19th-Century Teaching," in *The Puritans: Their Origins and Successors; Addresses Delivered at the Puritan and Westminster Conferences, 1959-1978* (Carlisle, PA: Banner of Truth Trust, 1987), 316.

How Christians Should Deal with Sin

There are at least three main views on how Christians should deal with sin:

1. *Instantly eradicate sin.* This is Wesley's Christian perfectionism (see "Wesleyan Perfectionism: Perfect Love toward God and Humans" in chap. 1).

2. *Continuously counteract sin.* This is higher life theology (see "Day 1. The Diagnosis: Sin" in chap. 2).

3. *Kill sin as the Holy Spirit gradually transforms you and restores God's image in you.* This is a process that God does not complete until he glorifies you. The process is not uniformly gradual—it may include growth spurts and backsliding. This is the Reformed view of progressive sanctification (see fig. 3.8).

The key issue is what happens to the whole person. If you are a Christian, does your sinful part remain completely unchanged until God glorifies you? Or does God transform your whole person so that you progressively— though not completely—triumph over sin?

That raises a controversial issue: What is the sinful "part" of a Christian?

Old Self vs. New Self; Old Nature vs. New Nature

Before you became a Christian, your "old self" was in Adam and served sin (Rom 6:6; Col 3:9; cf. Eph 4:22). As a Christian, your "new self" is in Christ and serves Christ (Col 3:10; cf. Eph 4:24). Neither "old self" nor "new self" refers to a part of you; it refers to your whole person.

Your old self had only one nature, but your new self is more complex. Does a Christian have one nature or two? It depends on how you define *nature*.[3] If you define nature as a complex of attributes, then it makes sense to distinguish your sinful nature from your new nature. The one-nature and two-nature views are practically identical because both acknowledge a conflict between "two opposing somethings—principles, desires, urgings, etc." in the Christian.[4] Two-nature advocates call them *natures*.[5] One-nature advocates describe these two aspects of the Christian's one

---

3. William W. Combs, "Does the Believer Have One Nature or Two?," *Detroit Baptist Seminary Journal* 2 (1997): 81.

4. Ibid., 86.

5. Anthony A. Hoekema, *Saved by Grace* (Grand Rapids: Eerdmans, 1989), 209–14.

nature as "two struggling principles,"[6] "two opposed sorts of desire,"[7] or "contrary urgings."[8]

THREE PROBLEMS WITH HOW HIGHER LIFE THEOLOGY VIEWS SIN IN THE CHRISTIAN

Problem 1: Higher life theology misunderstands the nature of the flesh. The problem with higher life theology is not that it refers to two natures in a Christian but that it incorrectly understands the flesh to be an equally powerful nature alongside the believer's new nature. According to higher life theology, both natures are unchanging entities within the Christian, and only one is in total control at any given moment. Thus, the flesh either controls the believer, or the Spirit is counteracting the flesh. A Christian in "category 1" (see fig. 2.3) lives "in the flesh." It is all or nothing. A Christian is either "in the flesh" or "in the Spirit." The two natures are two opposing principles that vie for supremacy, like two fierce dogs: if a Christian feeds the good dog and starves the bad dog, then the good dog wins. Christians in "category 1" feed their flesh, which dominates their life and produces a fleshly lifestyle. For Christians in "category 2," the Spirit counteracts their sinful nature with the result that they prevail over all known sin.

The NT uses σάρξ (*sarx*, "flesh") in many different senses.[9] The flesh is the realm in which non-Christians live (Rom 7:5; 8:4, 9; Eph 2:3; 1 John

---

6. John H. Gerstner, *Wrongly Dividing the Word of Truth: A Critique of Dispensationalism* (Brentwood, TN: Wolgemuth & Hyatt, 1991), 232.

7. Packer, *Keep in Step*, 33.

8. J. I. Packer, *Concise Theology: A Guide to Historic Christian Beliefs* (Wheaton, IL: Tyndale House, 1995), 171. Cf. Combs, "Does the Believer Have One Nature or Two?," 86: "The difference between one-nature and two-nature terminology is not over the *meaning* of the term *nature* but rather the *usage* of *nature* to describe different complexes of attributes. The value and attraction of two-nature terminology is that it provides convenient terminology to describe the struggle with sin within every believer. Those who decry the idea of two-natures in the believer would still strongly affirm that struggle, but they simply believe that it is not theologically accurate to describe it as a struggle between the old and new natures. Such terminology, they feel, can be misleading."

9. See Andrew David Naselli, *Let Go and Let God? A Survey and Analysis of Keswick Theology* (Bellingham, WA: Lexham Press, 2010), 321–23 ("Appendix D: A Word Study on ΣΑΡΞ [Flesh]"); Naselli, *How to Understand and Apply the New Testament: Twelve Steps*

2:15–16).[10] Christians do not live in the flesh in that sense because people who live in the flesh fail to inherit the kingdom of God (Gal 5:19–21). But Christians battle against the flesh (Gal 5:16–17, 24; cf. 1 Pet 2:11). The flesh is not like a dog that the Christian can weaken and possibly kill by starving it, nor is the flesh an equal opponent to the Spirit, who opposes the flesh and ultimately triumphs over it. Rather, the flesh is the Christian's sinful disposition, and the Christian and the Spirit progressively mortify its sinful deeds.

Problem 2: Higher life theology rejects that the Holy Spirit gradually transforms the whole Christian. Higher life theology teaches that Christians must continuously *counteract* sin. It views a Christian as having two natures that cannot improve. But the Spirit does not merely counteract sin in you without dealing with the sin principle. The Spirit transforms your whole person—not just one part of you. You become increasingly holy and less sinful as the Holy Spirit enables you to kill sin.[11]

Problem 3: Higher life theology has a low view of sin. "Wrong views about holiness are generally traceable to wrong views about human corruption."[12] Higher life theology teaches that you can be free of *known* sin, but that is "an imperfect perfection, perfect only to the Christian's consciousness."[13]

---

from *Exegesis to Theology* (Phillipsburg, NJ: P&R Publishing, 2017), 221–24 ("Example: σάρξ [*Sarx*, Flesh] and πνεῦμα [*Pneuma*, Spirit]").

10. F. F. Bruce, *Paul: Apostle of the Heart Set Free* (Grand Rapids: Eerdmans, 1977), 209: "To be 'in the Spirit' is for Paul the opposite of being 'in the flesh.' All believers, according to him, are 'in the Spirit.'"

11. Benjamin B. Warfield, "The Victorious Life," in *Perfectionism: Volume II*, vol. 8 of *The Works of Benjamin B. Warfield* (New York: Oxford University Press, 1932), 580. The Holy Spirit "cures our sinning by curing our sinful nature; He makes the tree good that the fruit may be good. It is, in other words, precisely by eradicating our sinfulness—'the corruption of our hearts'—that He delivers us from sinning. ... We cannot be saved from sinning except as we are saved from sin; and the degree in which we are saved from sinning is the index of the degree in which we have been saved from sin." On killing sin, see John Owen, "Of the Mortification of Sin in Believers," in *Overcoming Sin and Temptation*, ed. Kelly M. Kapic and Justin Taylor (Wheaton, IL: Crossway, 2006), 37–139.

12. J. C. Ryle, *Holiness: Its Nature, Hindrances, Difficulties, and Roots, Being a Series of Papers on the Subject*, 4th ed. (London: Hunt, 1889), 1.

13. Benjamin B. Warfield, "The 'Higher Life' Movement," in *Perfectionism: Volume II*, vol. 8 of *The Works of Benjamin B. Warfield* (New York: Oxford University Press, 1932), 527.

Sin is not limited to sinful actions that you are aware of: "Sin is lack of conformity to the moral law of God, either in act, disposition, or state."[14] The human heart is deceitful and desperately sick *beyond cure* (Jer 17:9). And the more you mature as a Christian, the more sensitive you will become to how sinful you are. The more holy you become, the more you will see your sin. Paul himself increasingly realized his own sinfulness, referring to himself as "the least of the apostles" (1 Cor 15:9), then "the very least of all the saints" (Eph 3:8), and finally, "the foremost" of "sinners" (1 Tim 1:15). Although all believers experience "a real and genuine (actual) victory, it is a qualified victory" because it does not consist in victory over all known sin.[15] "Reformed theologians ... constantly affirm that the Christian's best works are never so good that his conscience ceases to tell him that they could and should have been better."[16]

REASON 3. A FORM OF QUIETISM
It Emphasizes Passivity, Not Activity

Higher life theology's quietism is evident in the slogan "Let go and let God," which "is the essence of the teaching."[17] The "let" idea emphasizes passivity and discourages activity.[18] Victorious Christian living is "the Christ-life," in which Christ literally lives a Christian's life for that Christian. Frances Havergal's hymn "Church of God, Beloved and Chosen" captures that passivity with the phrase "Holiness by faith in Jesus, not by effort of my own."

---

14. Augustus Hopkins Strong, *Systematic Theology: A Compendium and Commonplace Book Designed for the Use of Theological Students*, 3 vols. (Philadelphia: American Baptist Publication Society, 1907), 549.

15. William W. Combs, "The Disjunction between Justification and Sanctification in Contemporary Evangelical Theology," *Detroit Baptist Seminary Journal* 6 (2001): 43.

16. J. I. Packer, "Keswick and the Reformed Doctrine of Sanctification," *Evangelical Quarterly* 27 (1955): 163.

17. Lloyd-Jones, "Living the Christian Life," 319. The largest quietistic influence on higher life theology comes from Robert Pearsall Smith and his wife, Hannah. Both the Smiths grew up as Quakers, and Hannah's quietism reflects Quaker doctrine. Robert Wilson, who cofounded the Keswick Convention, was also a Quaker.

18. David D. Cho, "The Old Princeton Presbyterian Response to the Holiness Movement in the Late Nineteenth and Twentieth Centuries in America" (PhD diss., Westminster Theological Seminary, 1994), 207: "Keswick's emphasis lies in the notion of a 'resting faith' which would inevitably promote passivity and quietism."

> Quietism ... holds that all initiatives on our part, of any sort, are the energy of the flesh; that God will move us, if at all, by inner promptings and constraints that are recognizably not thoughts and impulses of our own; and that we should always be seeking the annihilation of our selfhood so that divine life may flow freely through our physical frames. ... Passivity means conscious inaction—in this case [i.e., with higher life theology], inner inaction. A call to passivity—conscientious, consecrated passivity—has sometimes been read into certain biblical texts, but it cannot be read out of any of them.[19]

The New Testament teaches that Christians are responsible to actively pursue holiness:

1. *Progressive sanctification involves a lifelong struggle.* "The desires of the flesh are against the Spirit, and the desires of the Spirit are against the flesh, for these are opposed to each other, to keep you from doing the things you want to do" (Gal 5:17; see 5:16–26). "The passions of the flesh," asserts Peter, "wage war against your soul" (1 Pet 2:11).[20]

2. *Progressive sanctification requires active effort.*[21] Christians must become what they are. All Christians are saints in the sense that they are *already holy* (definitive sanctification), and God's holy people must *become holy* (progressive sanctification). (See fig. 4.1.)

---

19. Packer, *Keep in Step*, 127–28.
20. Another passage that may support this theme is Romans 7:14–25. Scholars debate whether that passage refers to Christians or non-Christians. See Naselli, *Let Go and Let God?*, 272–74.
21. E.g., see Rom 12–13; 1 Cor 9:24; 2 Cor 7:1; Gal 5:13–17; Eph 4–6; Phil 3:12–17; 4:4–9; Col 3:1–4:6; 1 Thess 5:8–22; 1 Tim 4:7–10; 6:11–12; Heb 12:1–3, 14–16; 1 Pet 1:13–25; 2:11–18; 2 Pet 1:5–7; 3:14–18.

Fig. 4.1. Illustrations of How Christians Must Become What They Are

What You Are	Become What You Are
"We know that our old self was crucified with him in order that the body of sin might be brought to nothing, so that we would no longer be enslaved to sin" (Rom 6:6)	"So you also must consider yourselves dead to sin and alive to God in Christ Jesus" (Rom 6:11)
"you who were once slaves of sin … having been set free from sin, have become slaves of righteousness" (Rom 6:17–18)	"present your members as slaves to righteousness leading to sanctification" (Rom 6:19)
"To the church of God that is in Corinth, to those sanctified in Christ Jesus, called to be saints" (1 Cor 1:2); "God's temple is holy, and you are that temple" (1 Cor 3:17); "your body is a temple of the Holy Spirit within you" (1 Cor 6:19)	The gospel requires God's holy people to mature in purity (1 Corinthians); e.g., "So glorify God in your body" (1 Cor 6:20)
"as you really are unleavened" (1 Cor 5:7b)	"Cleanse out the old leaven that you may be a new lump" (1 Cor 5:7a)
"as many of you as were baptized into Christ have put on Christ" (Gal 3:27)	"put on the Lord Jesus Christ" (Rom 13:14a)
"those who belong to Christ Jesus have crucified the flesh with its passions and desires" (Gal 5:24)	"make no provision for the flesh, to gratify its desires" (Rom 13:14b)

Paul portrays the Christian life as warfare (Eph 6:10–18; 1 Tim 6:12). "*Walking* is one of Paul's favorite metaphors for spirituality" (cf. Rom 6:4; 8:4; 2 Cor 5:7; Gal 5:16; Eph 5:2; Col 1:10), and it is "an excellent metaphor for the Christian life because it implies progress, continual movement, and the development of strength."[22] Packer is right: "The Christian's motto should not be 'Let go and let God' but 'Trust God and get going!'"[23]

But while higher life theology is a form of quietism, it is also …

---

22. Larry D. Pettegrew, *The New Covenant Ministry of the Holy Spirit*, 2nd ed. (Grand Rapids: Kregel, 2001), 206–7.
23. Packer, *Keep in Step*, 128.

REASON 4. A FORM OF PELAGIANISM
It Portrays the Christian's Free Will as Autonomously Starting and Stopping Sanctification

Pelagianism exalts a human's autonomous free will and inherent ability to obey any of God's commands apart from God's help. It rejects that humans are totally depraved and affirms that human responsibility (*ought*) necessarily implies ability (*can*). In other words, if God commands humans to do something (e.g., "repent and believe" or "be perfect"), then humans must possess the inherent ability to obey that command without God's help.

Higher life theology is not pure Pelagianism, which is heresy. But higher life theology is a *form* of Pelagianism because one factor decisively determines whether a Christian is in category 1 or 2 (see fig. 2.3): It ultimately depends on the Christian's free will.[24] So ultimately, Christians are in control of their sanctification. Their will is decisive in starting and stopping progressive sanctification.

In reply:

1. *Your will is not autonomously free.* Your will is free only in the sense that you are free to act according to your nature.[25]
2. *You work because God works.* According to higher life theology, God does all the work, and you are passive—with one crucial condition: *You must choose to let God work.* That is why higher life theology is simultaneously both quietistic and Pelagian-like.[26] It encourages Christians to view God as a power tool that they just plug in so that God does all the work.

This is the Achilles heel of higher life theology: *When a Christian is in category 2 (see fig. 2.3), who is responsible when that person sins—Christ or the Christian?* No one would say Christ; it must be the Christian. But once a Christian surrenders himself completely to the indwelling Christ, he still has the inherent ability to un-surrender himself and take control back!

---

24. Packer, "Keswick and the Reformed Doctrine of Sanctification," 158: *"Keswick teaching is Pelagian through and through."*

25. See Andrew David Naselli, "Do We Have a Free Will?," *Thoughts on Theology*, August 26, 2009, www.andynaselli.com/do-we-have-a-free-will; Scott Christensen, *What about Free Will? Reconciling Our Choices with God's Sovereignty* (Phillipsburg, NJ: P&R Publishing, 2016).

26. Cf. Warfield, "The 'Higher Life' Movement," 522, 532.

Otherwise Christ would be responsible for the Christian's sin.[27] The Christian's free will, therefore, autonomously and decisively starts and stops sanctification. Lloyd-Jones logically concludes that according to higher life theology,

> The most important factor in sanctification is the abiding of the believer rather than the keeping power of Christ. In other words man according to this view, and in spite of the phrase "let go and let God," seems to play the most vital part in the process, for, without his abiding, Christ cannot keep him.[28]

Placing such ultimate control in the Christian, argues Warfield, resembles both Pelagianism and magic and thus dishonors God.[29] Packer agrees that higher life theology replaces "Pelagian activism" with "Pelagian quietism" and is "little better than magic."[30] According to the New Testament, "The Holy Spirit uses my faith and obedience (which he himself first works in me) to sanctify me," but according to higher life theology, "I use the Holy Spirit (whom God puts at my disposal) to sanctify myself." Thus, higher life theology "is not merely unscriptural; it is irreligious. ... It is *Pelagian*;

---

27. Cf. Warfield, "The Victorious Life," 585–97, 600–11.

28. David Martyn Lloyd-Jones, *Christ Our Sanctification* (London: Inter-Varsity Press, 1948), 20.

29. Warfield, "The Victorious Life," 608–10: "This is as express a Pelagianism as Pelagius' own. It is not the same Pelagianism as Pelagius' own. It substitutes faith for Pelagius' works and it draws on God for all saving operations. ... And it is something far worse than Pelagianism, something the affinities of which are with magic rather than religion, which supposes that the activities of God can be commanded by acts of men, even if these acts be acts of faith. It is the essence of magic as distinguished from religion that it places supernatural powers at the disposal of men for working effects of their own choosing. It cannot be overlooked that the whole tendency of the teaching of Mr. Trumbull and his coterie is to place God at the disposal of man, and to encourage man to use Him in order to obtain results which he cannot attain for himself. This is of course to stand things on their head, and in doing so to degrade God into merely the instrument which man employs to secure his objects. ... God stands always helplessly by until man calls Him into action by opening a channel into which His energies may flow. It sounds dreadfully like turning on the steam or the electricity. ... Everywhere and always the initiative belongs to man; everywhere and always God's action is suspended upon man's will. ... It is nothing less than degrading to God to suppose Him thus subject to the control of man and unable to move except as man permits Him to do so."

30. Packer, "Keswick and the Reformed Doctrine of Sanctification," 154, 160–62.

for, in effect, it makes the Christian the employer, and the Holy Spirit the employee, in the work of sanctification."[31]

Progressive sanctification "is inevitable, though it is not automatic; it involves our 'responsible participation.'"[32] Although you participate, God, who began the process, is the one who energizes you and guarantees that he will complete what he began. You work *because* God works: "work out your own salvation with fear and trembling, for it is God who works in you, both to will and to work for his good pleasure" (Phil 2:12–13).

> God's working in us is not suspended because we work, nor our working suspended because God works. Neither is the relation strictly one of co-operation as if God did his part and we did ours so that the conjunction or coordination of both produced the required result. God works in us and we also work. But the relation is that *because* God works we work. All working out of salvation on our part is the effect of God's working in us, not the willing to the exclusion of the doing and not the doing to the exclusion of the willing, but both the willing and the doing. ... The more persistently active we are in working, the more persuaded we may be that all the energizing grace and power is of God. ... Sanctification is the sanctification of persons, and persons are not machines.[33]

REASON 5. MISREADING
It Does Not Interpret and Apply the Bible Accurately

Higher life theology misinterprets and misapplies the Bible. Here are three examples:

1. It assumes that the Greek aorist tense-form indicates point-in-time action, especially with reference to proof texts for the crisis of consecration (e.g., Rom 6:13; 12:1). That is an exegetical fallacy. Standard Greek grammars as well as recent studies on verbal aspect deny that the aorist tense-form must or even usually refers

---

31. Ibid., 162, 166.
32. Combs, "Disjunction," 43.
33. John Murray, *Redemption: Accomplished and Applied* (Grand Rapids: Eerdmans, 1955), 148–50.

to point-in-time action, affirming instead that the aorist tense-form is the default tense that communicates in the most general way possible.[34]

2. It interprets the Bible allegorically, especially in narrative literature, to make theological points regarding the Christian life.

> Instead of expounding the great New Testament texts, they so often started with their theory and illustrated it by means of Old Testament characters and stories. You will find that so often their texts were Old Testament texts. Indeed their method of teaching was based on the use of illustrations rather than on exposition of Scripture. An inevitable result was that they virtually ignored everything that had been taught on the subject of sanctification during the previous eighteen centuries. That is not merely my statement. Many of them boasted of this.[35]

For example, Harford-Battersby, cofounder of the Keswick Convention, converted to "the deeper life" when he heard a sermon on John 4:46–50 that distinguished between the nobleman's "seeking faith" (category 1) and "resting faith" (category 2).

3. It emphasizes experience at the expense of doctrine. Robert Pearsall Smith helped set this tone when he led a higher life meeting: "We did not come to Oxford to set each other right, or to discuss doctrines."[36] Hannah Whitall Smith uses the same tone by opening her most influential work—which addresses the deeply theological issue of progressive sanctification—with a disclaimer that downplays theology and appeals to experience.[37] One Keswick historian explains,

---

34. See Andrew David Naselli, "A Brief Introduction to Verbal Aspect Theory in New Testament Greek," *Detroit Baptist Seminary Journal* 12 (2007): 17–28.

35. Lloyd-Jones, "Living the Christian Life," 321.

36. Robert Pearsall Smith, ed., *Account of the Union Meeting for the Promotion of Scriptural Holiness, Held at Oxford August 29 to September 7, 1874* (London: Daldy, Isbister, 1875), 59.

37. Hannah Whitall Smith, *The Christian's Secret of a Happy Life*, 2nd ed. (Boston: Christian Witness, 1885), iii–iv.

> Keswick is interested in the practical application of religious truth rather than in doctrinal or dogmatic theology. ... The Convention is not interested in academic discussions of theology and ethics, or even in adding to the store of Bible knowledge of those who attend, but simply and only in helping men to be holy.[38]

"Perhaps this," responds Packer, "is the very unconcern that has caused the trouble. After all, Pelagianism is the natural heresy of zealous Christians who are not interested in theology."[39]

Pitting doctrine against devotion is a false dichotomy because God intends them to go together. They are not mutually exclusive; one without the other is incomplete.[40] Truth is truth proportionally; what you emphasize and deemphasize is significant. Higher life theology emphasizes that Christians should be holy. That is good. But it errs primarily by emphasizing a crisis of consecration and Spirit-filling that chronologically separates justification and progressive sanctification. That is the essential message of higher life theology, and it neither proportionately nor accurately reflects what the New Testament teaches about Christian living.

REASON 6. FALSE ASSURANCE
It Assures Spurious "Christians" They Are Saved

Higher life theology undermines the doctrines of perseverance and assurance by dividing Christians into two distinct categories.[41] But all genuine

---

38. Steven Barabas, *So Great Salvation: The History and Message of the Keswick Convention* (Westwood, NJ: Revell, 1952), 42, 108.

39. Packer, "Keswick and the Reformed Doctrine of Sanctification," 167.

40. Warfield strikes an outstanding balance in five articles in his *Selected Shorter Writings*, ed. John E. Meeter, 2 vols. (Phillipsburg, NJ: P&R Publishing, 1970–1973), which I list here chronologically: "Authority, Intellect, Heart," 2:668–71; "The Indispensableness of Systematic Theology to the Preacher," 2:280–88; "Spiritual Culture in the Theological Seminary," 2:468–96; "The Religious Life of Theological Students," 1:411–25; "The Purpose of the Seminary," 1:374–78.

41. On perseverance and assurance, see Donald S. Whitney, *How Can I Be Sure I'm a Christian? What the Bible Says about Assurance of Salvation* (Colorado Springs, CO: NavPress, 1994); D. A. Carson, "Reflections on Assurance," in *Still Sovereign: Contemporary Perspectives on Election, Foreknowledge, and Grace*, ed. Thomas R. Schreiner and Bruce A. Ware (Grand Rapids: Baker Books, 2000), 247–76; Sam Storms, *Kept*

Christians persevere in the faith. That is, genuine Christians can neither totally nor finally fall away from trusting Jesus (John 8:31; Heb 3:14; 1 John 4:15; 5:1), affirming sound doctrine (John 7:17; Col 1:22–23; 1 John 4:6), or doing good works (John 10:27; Eph 2:10). Christians continue or persevere to the end. The warning passages in Scripture are God-ordained means for believers to persevere. Both believers and unbelievers must beware of false faith (Matt 7:21–23; 1 Cor 9:27).

All genuine Christians persevere, but not all of them have assurance—and some non-Christians have false assurance. If you have assurance, you are convinced that you have eternal life—that you are a born-again Christian. And you can have different degrees of assurance (see fig. 4.2).

Fig. 4.2. Degrees of Assurance[42]

Non-Christian		?	Christian	
1. Strong evidence of unbelief	2. Weak evidence of unbelief	3. Mixed evidence of unbelief and faith	4. Weak evidence of faith	5. Strong evidence of faith
Should have no assurance to a stronger degree than #2	Should have no assurance to a weaker degree than #1 and a stronger degree than #3	Should have no assurance to a weaker degree than #2	Should have assurance to a weaker degree than #5	Should have assurance to a stronger degree than #4

◄───►

Strong degree of no assurance   Strong degree of assurance

The question mark in the middle column indicates that we simply cannot know whether such a person is a Christian. They may profess to be a Christian, but they should not have assurance that they are a Christian because the evidence is mixed.

---

for Jesus: What the New Testament Really Teaches about Assurance of Salvation and Eternal Security (Wheaton, IL: Crossway, 2015); Wayne Grudem, "Free Grace" Theology: 5 Ways It Diminishes the Gospel (Wheaton, IL: Crossway, 2016), 77–97.
42. This diagram adapts Grudem, "Free Grace" Theology, 92.

The *basis* of assurance is objective: It is based solely on Christ's finished cross-work as the word of God reveals. The *means* of assurance is subjective: You can know you are a Christian by the Holy Spirit's ongoing work in your life (e.g., Rom 8:14–17) and by your persevering in the faith (e.g., 1 John).[43]

A major problem with higher life theology is that rather than causing professing Christians to examine themselves to see whether they are genuine Christians persevering in the faith (2 Cor 13:5), it exhorts them to move from category 1 to category 2 (see fig. 2.3). A disastrous result of dividing Christians into those two distinct categories is that higher life theology can have a comforting, soothing effect on professing Christians who are not actually genuine Christians. Such a person might think, "I'm a carnal Christian, not a spiritual Christian. But I'm still on my way to heaven." Higher life theology gives such a person false assurance. A spurious "Christian" should not have assurance that they have eternal life. For example, if a sinful lifestyle characterizes you—such as unrepentantly indulging in pornography or immoral sex—then you should question whether you are really a Christian.[44]

Furthermore, if a person identifies as a "carnal Christian" in category 1, on what basis can a church excommunicate a so-called brother or sister?

> To have two classes of Christians makes the biblical commands to exercise church discipline difficult or impossible to apply. If Christians walk exactly like non-Christians, then the only way we could distinguish Christians from non-Christians would be by their profession of faith, not by their life. Yet Scripture makes clear that we are to exercise discipline on the basis of the walk of professing believers.[45]

---

43. Cf. Christopher D. Bass, *That You May Know: Assurance of Salvation in 1 John*, NAC Studies in Bible and Theology 5 (Nashville: Broadman & Holman, 2008).

44. Andrew David Naselli, "Seven Reasons You Should Not Indulge in Pornography," *Themelios* 41 (2016): 473–83.

45. Kenneth S. Kantzer, "A Reformed View of Sanctification," in *Free and Fulfilled: Victorious Living in the 21st Century*, ed. Robertson McQuilkin (Nashville: Nelson, 1997), 217. On church membership and discipline, see Jonathan Leeman, *Church Membership: How the World Knows Who Represents Jesus*, 9Marks (Wheaton, IL: Crossway, 2012); Leeman, *Church Discipline: How the Church Protects the Name of Jesus*,

REASON 7. METHODOLOGY

It Uses Superficial Formulas for Instantaneous Sanctification

The sermons and writings that employ higher life theology often have multistep formulas. For example, what are the conditions for experiencing Spirit-filling?

- Evan Hopkins gives four steps.
- J. Elder Cumming gives three steps.
- F. B. Meyer gives five conditions.
- Andrew Murray gives two conditions in one book, four steps in another, and seven steps in another.[46]

Such formulas are superficial because they are not the result of carefully reading and explaining the New Testament. The formulaic approach is common probably because it appeals to people who want simple applications and instant victory over sin. They deeply want to be more holy, and they are impatient with their struggle against sin and want God to deliver them from that struggle *now*. Superficial formulas seem like the recipe they are looking for—a shortcut to instantly conquering sin.

REASON 8. ADDICTION

It Fosters Dependency on Experiences at Special Holiness Meetings

The Keswick Convention saw itself as a spiritual clinic for Christians, but many of the same patients consistently returned year after year. One reason for that cycle is that Christians who embraced higher life theology became addicted to what they experienced at special holiness meetings. They made short-lived commitments in emotionally charged atmospheres—like the adult version of so-called "camp decisions" by young people.

> [Higher life theology] tends to make people dependent upon meetings and the particular atmosphere of certain meetings. Having surrendered at first in the highly charged emotional atmosphere of a meeting, and having received the bless-

---

9Marks (Wheaton, IL: Crossway, 2012); John S. Hammett and Benjamin L. Merkle, eds., *Those Who Must Give an Account: A Study of Church Membership and Church Discipline* (Nashville: Broadman & Holman, 2012); Jeremy M. Kimble, *40 Questions about Church Membership and Church Discipline*, 40 Questions (Grand Rapids: Kregel, 2017).
46. See Naselli, *Let Go and Let God?*, 209–12.

ing, they subsequently seemed to lose it, and were unable to regain it until they found themselves once more in the same atmosphere. This process is repeated several times and often leads to a type of life strangely comparable to that of an electric battery which constantly runs down and has to be re-charged by a dynamo. Religious meetings and gatherings are invaluable aids to the Christian life, but when we live by them and become entirely dependent upon them and begin to think that we must wait for them before we can live the Christian life as we ought to live it, they become the very snare of the devil.[47]

This phenomenon also repeats itself in public invitations or "altar calls" that some preachers regularly give to Christians at the end of a sermon.[48] The same tender-hearted Christians often respond repeatedly to such appeals, developing a mindset that real sanctification takes place when you publicly "walk the aisle" for "reconsecration" or "rededication." That approach can be counterproductive because it does not train Christians to pursue steady, progressive growth through the means of grace such as Bible intake, prayer, worship, evangelism, serving, and stewardship.[49]

REASON 9. ABUSE
It Frustrates and Disillusions the Have-Nots

Higher life theology ultimately disillusions believers in their progressive sanctification because it presents an unattainable standard. It's impossible for us to live free from sin.

Christians who follow higher life theology—mainly because they deeply desire to be holy—often become frustrated and dangerously dis-

---

47. Lloyd-Jones, *Christ Our Sanctification*, 19.

48. On the altar call, see Iain H. Murray, *The Invitation System* (Edinburgh: Banner of Truth Trust, 1967); Murray, *Revival and Revivalism: The Making and Marring of American Evangelicalism 1750-1858* (Carlisle, PA: Banner of Truth Trust, 1994); David Bennett, *The Altar Call: Its Origin and Present Usage* (New York: University Press of America, 2000).

49. Cf. Donald S. Whitney, *Spiritual Disciplines for the Christian Life*, 2nd ed. (Colorado Springs, CO: NavPress, 2014).

illusioned. And that can result in brutal experiences.[50] Such Christians may morbidly introspect and repeat "an endless cycle that looks something like the following":

1. I need to be victorious.
2. If I consecrate myself, I will be victorious.
3. I now consecrate myself.
4. I am not victorious; therefore, I did not consecrate myself sufficiently.
5. Go back to number one. ...

> DYSFUNCTIONAL LIVING: In the final analysis, Christians who remain in the Higher Life "syndrome" must eventually distort reality. The truth is that they are *not* victorious over sin and that they are *not* all that holy. If they refuse to accept this fact, they must redefine such things as sin, righteousness, maturity, repentance, revival, and even the Gospel itself. Moreover, their view of themselves must continually be skewed. That can be the start of serious mental and emotional disaster. Christians must live and walk in *truth* about God and themselves.[51]

God uses different means to rescue his disillusioned people from higher life theology. For me, that included counsel and preaching from pastors (especially Mike Harding and Mark Minnick) and books and articles by theologians both dead (especially Martyn Lloyd-Jones, John Murray, John Owen, J. C. Ryle, B. B. Warfield) and alive (especially D. A. Carson, William Combs, Sinclair Ferguson, Wayne Grudem, John MacArthur, Rolland

---

50. One example is Mark Rathe. In 1974, he traveled worldwide as an assistant to higher life advocate Major Ian Thomas, but at the end of his travels, Rathe felt confused, unfulfilled, frustrated, and spiritually defeated rather than victorious. See Mark Steven Rathe, "The Keswick Movement: Its Origins and Teachings" (MA thesis, Simpson College, 1987), 3-4, 88-94.

51. Philip L. Smuland, "Introduction," in The *"Higher Life" Doctrine of Sanctification, Tried by the Word of God*, by Henry A. Boardman (1877; repr., Harrisonburg, VA: Sprinkle, 1996), x-xi.

McCune, J. I. Packer, and John Piper). For Albert Martin, it was J. C. Ryle's *Holiness.*[52] For J. I. Packer, it was John Owen.

Packer's testimony is moving.[53] Higher life theology frustrated the tender-hearted Packer as a young, recent convert when he pursued holiness. "It didn't work," Packer recounts, "and that was a deeply frustrating and depressing thing. It made me feel like a pariah, an outsider, and at the age of eighteen that was pretty burdensome. In fact, it was driving me crazy."[54] He testifies, "The reality of [higher life theology's] passivity program and its announced expectations, plus its insistence that any failure to find complete victory is entirely your fault, makes it very destructive. I know this; I have been at the receiving end of it."[55]

Packer felt like a "poor drug addict" desperately, unsuccessfully, and painfully trying "to walk through a brick wall." The explanation for his struggle, according to higher life theology, was his "unwillingness to pay the entry fee," that is, he didn't fully consecrate himself. "So all he could do was repeatedly reconsecrate himself, scraping the inside of his psyche till it was bruised and sore in order to track down still un-yielded things by which the blessing was perhaps being blocked." His confusion, frustra-

---

52. Albert N. Martin, "The Theological Basis of Mortification," in *Sanctification: Growing in Grace*, ed. Joseph A. Pipa Jr. and J. Andrew Wortman (Taylors, SC: Southern Presbyterian, 2001), 86.

53. See J. I. Packer, preface to *Holiness: Its Nature, Hindrances, Difficulties, and Roots*, by J. C. Ryle, centenary ed. (Welwyn: Evangelical, 1979), vii–viii; Packer, *Keep in Step*, 128–30 (cf. 92); Packer, introduction to *Sin and Temptation: The Challenge of Personal Godliness*, by John Owen, ed. James M. Houston, Classics of Faith and Devotion (Minneapolis: Bethany House, 1996), xvii–xxx, esp. xxv–xxix; Alister E. McGrath, *J. I. Packer: A Biography* (Grand Rapids: Baker, 1997), 22–26, 76–80; Wendy Murray Zoba, "Knowing Packer: The Lonely Journey of a Passionate Puritan," *Christianity Today* 42, no. 4 (1998): 30–40, esp. 33; Jeffrey P. Greenman, "Packer, James Innell," in *Biographical Dictionary of Evangelicals*, ed. Timothy T. Larsen (Downers Grove, IL: InterVarsity Press, 2003), 497; John H. Armstrong, "A Reformation and Revival Journal Interview with James I. Packer," *Reformation and Revival* 13, no. 4 (2004): 163–96, esp. 166–69; Sam Storms, *Packer on the Christian Life: Knowing God in Christ, Walking by the Spirit*, Theologians on the Christian Life (Wheaton, IL: Crossway, 2015), esp. 63–89; Leland Ryken, *J. I. Packer: An Evangelical Life* (Wheaton, IL: Crossway, 2015), 45–47, 93–94, 266–67, 382–83.

54. Armstrong, "Interview with James I. Packer," 169.

55. Packer, *Keep in Step*, 128.

tion, and pain grew as he kept "missing the bus." The pursuit was as futile as chasing a "will-o'-the-wisp." He felt like "a burned child" who "dreads the fire, and hatred of the cruel and tormenting unrealities of overheated holiness teaching remains in his heart to this day."[56] Packer concludes that higher life theology is depressing because it fails to eradicate any of the Christian's sin, and it is delusive because

> it offers a greater measure of deliverance from sin than Scripture anywhere promises or the apostles themselves ever attained. This cannot but lead either to self-deception, in the case of those who profess to have entered into this blessing, or to disillusionment and despair, in the case of those who seek it but fail to find it.[57]

Higher life theology fosters elitism among Christians. It schismatically divides Christians into the haves and the have-nots—those who experientially know the secret and those who do not. And that leaves the have-nots frustrated and disillusioned.

REASON 10. SPIN
It Misinterprets Personal Experiences

The previous nine critiques of higher life theology raise an important question: How do you explain it when God transforms Christians who testify that higher life theology is the cause? The answer is not to deny that God genuinely transformed them. The answer is that such people theologically misinterpret their personal experiences.[58] Some believers take such a large step of growth at one time that they remember it for years. The error is in calling that large step of growth a once-for-all-time "crisis" that enables "real" progressive sanctification to begin. Some believers experience multiple large steps of growth, and others experience more gradual steps.[59]

---

56. Ibid., 129. (Packer wrote his testimony in the third person.)
57. Packer, "Keswick and the Reformed Doctrine of Sanctification," 166.
58. John Piper, "Letter to a Friend Concerning the So-Called 'Lordship Salvation,'" *Desiring God*, February 1, 1990, www.desiringgod.org/articles/letter-to-a-friend-concerning-the-so-called-lordship-salvation.
59. Cf. Wayne Grudem, *Systematic Theology: An Introduction to Biblical Doctrine* (Grand Rapids: Zondervan, 1994), 752, 775–81.

A helpful analogy to this is eating. Do you remember *every* meal you've ever eaten? That's impossible. But you can probably recall *some* of them. One of my most memorable meals occurred on December 6, 2008, at Ruth's Chris Steakhouse. I had just finished a week of exhausting comprehensive exams at Trinity Evangelical Divinity School, and my wife and I decided to use a gift card at some restaurant I had never heard of. I didn't know steak could taste that good! You may remember for years certain meals that you have eaten, but you cannot remember most of the meals you have eaten. That does not mean that you have failed to eat meals consistently; it means that some meals were more memorable than others. Similarly, as Christians mature, some steps of spiritual growth may be more memorable than others.

> You may find Christians at every stage of this process, for it is a process through which all must pass; but you will find none who will not in God's own good time and way pass through every stage of it. There are not two kinds of Christians, although there are Christians at every conceivable stage of advancement towards the one goal to which all are bound and at which all shall arrive.[60]

Furthermore, some who hear higher life theology do not process all the theological inaccuracies. Instead, they benefit when the teaching emphasizes relying on Christ instead of relying on yourself.

> God is very gracious and truly gives himself to all who truly seek him (see Jer. 29:13; Acts 10:34–35), never mind whether their theology is good or not so good. … The devotional conclusion is that when Christians ask God to make them more like Jesus, through the Spirit's power, he will do it, never mind what shortcomings appear in their theology. He is a most gracious and generous God ….[61]

So should we give higher life theology a pass? I agree with Packer:

> Does any of this justify the inaccuracies of Keswick teaching? No. It is not much of a recommendation when all you

---

60. B. B. Warfield, review of *He That Is Spiritual*, by Lewis Sperry Chafer, *Princeton Theological Review* 17 (1919): 327.

61. Packer, *Keep in Step*, 129, 133.

can say is that this teaching may help you if you do not take its details too seriously. It is utterly damning to have to say, as in this case I think we must, that if you do take its details seriously, it will tend not to help you but to destroy you.[62]

---

62. Ibid., 130.

Conclusion

Bad theology dishonors God and hurts people. That's why I wrote this book evaluating higher life theology. I love God, and I don't want higher life theology to hurt people. Higher life theology hurt me, and it has hurt many others. Don't let that happen to you!

I almost gave this book a title that was too long—like an old-school Puritan title: Why "Let Go and Let God" Is a Bad Idea: or, Why Higher Life Theology's Quick Fix to Your Struggle with Sin Will Not Result in a Higher Life, Deeper Life, Victorious Life, More Abundant Life, or Anything Other Than a Misguided, Frustrated, Disillusioned, and/or Destroyed Life. But I settled on a more concise title: *No Quick Fix*. Higher life theology is a quick fix that doesn't work.

Higher life theology is commendable in some ways, but its harmful features far outweigh its positive ones:

1. It creates two categories of Christians.
2. It portrays a shallow and incomplete view of sin in the Christian life.
3. It emphasizes passivity, not activity.
4. It portrays the Christian's free will as autonomously starting and stopping sanctification.
5. It does not interpret and apply the Bible accurately.
6. It assures spurious "Christians" they are saved.
7. It uses superficial formulas for instantaneous sanctification.
8. It fosters dependency on experiences at special holiness meetings.
9. It frustrates and disillusions the have-nots.
10. It misinterprets personal experiences.

There is a better way. See the appendix: "A More Excellent Way: Recommended Resources on the Christian Life." I highlight resources for further study that avoid the harmful elements of higher life theology and will feed your soul and stir your affections for our glorious God.

But first, don't miss the afterword that concludes this book. John MacArthur has been faithfully teaching the Bible and critiquing higher life theology for about fifty years. I asked him if he would be willing to tell his own story regarding higher life theology (including the so-called "Lordship salvation" controversy) and evoke the joy and freedom of moving away from it and helping others do the same. John graciously agreed. His afterword creates an effective one-two punch with how I critique higher life theology in part 2, and it nicely bookends my own story in the introduction.

Afterword by John MacArthur

I was not raised on Reformed theology; far from it. I was raised under the influence of higher life theology without the title. Until I reached seminary, an uncritical acceptance of the various forms of this deceptive and frustrating credo was what I thought of as Christianity. Every Sunday, the post-sermon invitation the preacher gave included a call to dedication, rededication, consecration, or surrender. The assumption was clearly that there were two kinds of Christians: lower-level believers and those who had decided to give themselves more fully to the Lord. Believers who entered into this advanced level of commitment would shift from being carnal to being spiritual. They would thus enter into a state of almost effortless victory over sin and temptation.

Every guest preacher at our revival meetings, the annual Bible conference, and especially youth camp would end his talk with a passionate call for those who were just Christians to give up everything and follow the Lord. Often, if not always, camp ended with an invitation to rededicate our lives and demonstrate seriousness by coming to the front of the campfire meeting and throwing a stick in the fire. The stick was supposed to be the symbol of a life given fully to the Lord. There was lots of drama, some tears, and earnest hope that this act would be transformational. But those things inevitably were followed in a few days by frustration as the same struggle for holiness and victory began exactly where it left off before camp.

My beloved Dad, a faithful pastor and preacher, had filled the shelves of his study library with all the higher-plane, deeper-life, Keswick devotional authors (whom Naselli identifies in this book). They provided much material for his sermons, with the same emphasis, though somewhat muted. We all believed that praying a prayer of faith settled salvation. When a life didn't change, there was the need for consecration—the leap to the next level, where spirituality became sort of automatic as you "let go and let God" work by yielding to an unusual empowering by the Holy Spirit.

While still in high school, I was unsuccessfully chasing that elusive spiritual moment of surrender. I even read *Imitation of Christ* by Thomas à Kempis and *Power through Prayer* by E. M. Bounds, searching for the doorway to full victory in my conflict with sin. Deeper-life writers often used language with gnostic overtones—promising to reveal "the secret of victorious living" or "the key to a deeper life."

But I was not experiencing the victory that I thought I was supposed to. I was desirous of doing right and honorably did want to serve the Lord. But I was certain that I fell short of what the Lord desired and deserved. I spent years in pursuit of the mysterious formula that would instantly launch me onto that higher plane of sanctification.

A few years at a legalistic Christian college didn't help. I was active in ministry there, but found that keeping external rules for the sake of appearance cannot restrain the flesh. I saw that building a pious veneer with manmade rules actually produces hypocrisy. Under the surface of strict legalism and sanctimonious formality, there is always much evil. I left the school still looking for that true experience.

A violent, near-deadly automobile accident while in college put me in bed for months. I tried to draw on that trial as motivation to move up (higher) or down (deeper). I did learn that my life was not mine to control and that I needed to be far more serious with the things of the Lord, but I still wasn't sure how to get where I needed to be.

During my student days, Campus Crusade for Christ launched at UCLA and drew its theological breath from the brand of higher life teaching that separates the lordship of Christ from the gospel. Crusade mass-produced and distributed two booklets. One was a booklet on how to be saved, and the other was a booklet on how to be sanctified. Both were simplistic, formulaic fast-track steps to get the desired result. With the first book, you could become a carnal Christian. The second book told you how to become a spiritual Christian. The influence of Crusade was global. They popularized higher life teaching with tens of thousands of young people. The influence of Crusade drove a large number of young men out of secular universities into Dallas Theological Seminary.

Dallas Seminary was the academic bastion of this two-part view of salvation. That seminary made the view of the carnal Christian and the spiritual Christian seem doctrinally and intellectually acceptable. I experienced this kind of theology firsthand when I was invited twice to the seminary to do a week-long preaching series. Some years later when I understood more precisely how pervasive this teaching was and what damage it was doing, I decided to write some books targeting the error. I responded in particular to published works written by members of the faculty at Dallas Seminary. My books were entitled *The Gospel according to Jesus* and *The Gospel according to the Apostles*. This year will bring the publication of the third book in that series *The Gospel according to Paul*. All three books were born out of my concern for the confusion and deception spread by the errors of "no-lordship salvation."

On the personal side, I had several friends in high school, college, and seminary—professing Christians headed toward Christian ministry—who radically defected from the faith to engage in the pursuit of false religion, atheism, and immorality. I struggled to believe that they were low-level, carnal, unsanctified Christians still on their way to heaven, as those who advocate no-lordship doctrine would affirm.

With all this swirling in my mind, I chose to write my master's thesis in seminary on Judas Iscariot. I wanted to understand the condition of the defector versus that of a true believer. There in seminary for the first time I began to read Reformed theology and the Puritans. I also became serious about exegeting Scripture.

In the years after seminary, I continued to look back through my life and consider how many people I knew in my Dad's churches who identified as Christians, and yet their lives gave no evidence of genuine faith. I thought about friends of the family, relatives, board members, fellow students, youth ministers, and people in the congregations I had attended. Over the years I had known many dozens of people who claimed to be Christians but whose behavior and values were indistinguishable from my unbelieving neighbors. They lacked any evidence of grace in their lives. Most evangelicals had long since come to the point of embracing such "carnal Christians" as legitimate Christians despite their utter lack of any commitment to Christ. They assumed such people just needed to surrender to the Spirit.

Evangelists like Billy Graham had convinced thousands of aisle-walkers they were saved by that act of response. But only a miniscule percentage of them ever united with any church after the meetings ended. Their names may have gone to a church, but their bodies never followed.

In February 1969, this concern about true salvation led me to choose Matthew 7:21–23 as the text for my inaugural sermon as pastor of Grace Community Church. I gave the same warning to the church that our Lord gave at the end of his Sermon on the Mount—that many who claim to be Christians don't have a saving relationship with him at all. Such will be condemned to hell while claiming to have worked in his name. That sermon launched a kind of revolution among comfortable false Christians and true Christians who thought the issue was a matter of a second blessing.

Since that first Sunday, the tone and emphasis of my ministry has always been to make clear that there is only one kind of Christian: a person who has been justified and is being sanctified. True believers are transformed at conversion, and their lives manifest the presence and power of their Lord. *Sanctification begins at justification*—meaning there is no such thing as a fundamentally carnal, incorrigibly disobedient Christian who refuses to surrender to Christ as Lord. No issue has been more important in my studying, writing, preaching, and leading than understanding and making known the biblical truth that sanctification begins when a person is truly converted, and not at some later point when a "carnal Christian" finally decides to surrender more fully to Christ.

The higher life, deeper life, "let go and let God" Keswick doctrine in all its forms drains the truth from the biblical doctrines of regeneration and sanctification. It degrades the doctrine of regeneration by allowing unsanctified false believers to think they are saved when their lives declare that they are not. It mutilates the doctrine of sanctification and thereby allows sanctified true believers to think they are not being sanctified although their lives—and the word of God—declare that they are. In other words, the deeper-life doctrine is a lie that deceives both true believers and people who falsely profess faith in Christ. A right understanding of salvation and sanctification is the foundation of true gospel faith. Certainly nothing has been more important to me in my spiritual pilgrimage than being delivered from those early misunderstandings into the clear truth of Scripture.

—John MacArthur, Pastor-Teacher of Grace Community
Church in Sun Valley, California; President of The
Master's University and The Master's Seminary

A More Excellent Way: Recommended Resources on the Christian Life

---

After critiquing Wesleyan perfectionism and higher life theology, Martyn Lloyd-Jones issued a convicting challenge:

> The things about which [George Whitefield and John Wesley] agreed were more important, and they had much fellowship together during the last years of Whitefield's life. We must follow these men. There are these differences, and we must be clear about them. But let us examine ourselves. It is easy to denounce false holiness teaching; but what is your holiness teaching? Have you the same desire for holiness? These men suffered, and sacrificed much in order to be holy men. They may have been confused about doctrines at times, they may have confused "things that differ," but they were zealously concerned to be holy men of God, and many of them were concerned to have a holy and a pure church. There, we surely are with them, and agree with them; and if we criticize what they taught, let us make sure that we have, and can preach and practice, "a more excellent way."[1]

---

1. David Martyn Lloyd-Jones, "'Living the Christian Life'—New Developments in the 18th and 19th-Century Teaching," in *The Puritans: Their Origins and Successors; Addresses Delivered at the Puritan and Westminster Conferences, 1959–1978* (Carlisle, PA: Banner of Truth Trust, 1987), 325.

I don't want to end this book solely on a negative this-is-why-that-view-is-wrong note. There is a more excellent way, and I want to point you to resources for further study. These resources avoid the destructive elements of higher life theology and will help you fan the flame of holiness that God keeps ablaze in your heart. This prayer is a good place to start: "Father, please make me as holy as a saved sinner can be."[2]

1. Barrett, Michael P. V. *Complete in Him: A Guide to Understanding and Enjoying the Gospel.* 2nd ed. Grand Rapids: Reformation Heritage, 2017. See especially Barrett's chapter on sanctification (pp. 193–230).

2. Bridges, Jerry. *The Discipline of Grace: God's Role and Our Role in the Pursuit of Holiness.* 2nd ed. Colorado Springs, CO: NavPress, 2006. "Your worst days are never so bad that you are beyond the *reach* of God's grace. And your best days are never so good that you are beyond the *need* of God's grace" (p. 19). See also Bridges's other books, including *The Gospel for Real Life: Turn to the Liberating Power of the Cross ... Every Day* (2003), *Respectable Sins: Confronting the Sins We Tolerate* (2007), *The Pursuit of Holiness* (2009), and *The Transforming Power of the Gospel* (2012).

3. Bunyan, John. *The Pilgrim's Progress.* 1678. Masterfully portrays how progressive sanctification requires active effort (see reason 3 in chap. 4 above: "A Form of Quietism"). Charles Spurgeon read Bunyan's classic over one hundred times. It's a pity that many Christians today have not read it even once. For some versions that my family enjoys, see www.andynaselli.com/pilgrims-progress-children.

4. Carson, D. A. Books, articles, sermons, interviews, etc. The Gospel Coalition lists Carson's publications and makes over 300 of the items available as free PDFs: www.thegospelcoalition.org/pages/d-a-carson-publications. I suggest starting with Carson's devotionals: *For the Love of God: A Daily Companion for Discovering the Riches of God's Word*, vols. 1–2 (Wheaton, IL: Crossway, 1998–1999). Then *The Cross and Christian Ministry: Leadership Lessons from 1 Cor-*

---

2. Cf. Andrew A. Bonar, *Memoir and Remains of the Rev. Robert Murray M'Cheyne* (Edinburgh: Oliphant, Anderson & Ferrier, 1894), 163: "In [M'Cheyne's] letters there are such expressions as these: 'I often pray, Lord, make me as holy as a pardoned sinner can be made.'"

inthians (Grand Rapids: Baker Books, 1993); "Reflections on Assurance," in *Still Sovereign: Contemporary Perspectives on Election, Foreknowledge, and Grace*, ed. Thomas R. Schreiner and Bruce A. Ware (Grand Rapids: Baker Books, 2000), 247–76; *Scandalous: The Cross and Resurrection of Jesus* (Wheaton, IL: Crossway, 2010); and *Praying with Paul: A Call to Spiritual Reformation*, 2nd ed. (Grand Rapids: Baker Academic, 2015).

5. Chapell, Bryan. *Holiness by Grace: Delighting in the Joy That Is Our Strength*. Wheaton, IL: Crossway, 2001. Explains principles of grace, practices of faith, and motives of love.

6. DeYoung, Kevin. *The Hole in Our Holiness: Filling the Gap between Gospel Passion and the Pursuit of Godliness*. Wheaton, IL: Crossway, 2012. Emphasizes what some who hold a Reformed view of sanctification tend not to emphasize: effort—Spirit-powered, gospel-driven, faith-fueled effort. My favorite section is where DeYoung lists forty ways "the Bible motivates us to pursue holiness" (pp. 57–60).

7. Ferguson, Sinclair. *In Christ Alone: Living the Gospel-Centered Life*. Orlando: Reformation Trust, 2007. Introduction to Christian living. See also Ferguson's "The Reformed View," in *Christian Spirituality: Five Views of Sanctification*, ed. Donald Alexander (Downers Grove, IL: InterVarsity Press, 1988), 47–76; and *Devoted to God: Blueprints for Sanctification* (Carlisle, PA: Banner of Truth Trust, 2016).

8. Grudem, Wayne. *Systematic Theology: An Introduction to Biblical Doctrine*. Grand Rapids: Zondervan, 1994. Well-organized, easy-to-understand, usually persuasive, and devotional. See especially the chapters on progressive sanctification, Spirit-baptism, and Spirit-filling (pp. 746–87; see also 788–809, 840–50). There are also two shorter versions of Grudem's systematic theology: the middle-level version is called *Bible Doctrine: Essential Teachings of the Christian Faith* (ed. Jeff Purswell; 1999), and the most condensed version is called *Christian Beliefs: Twenty Basics Every Christian Should Know* (ed. Elliot Grudem; 2005). Grudem is currently preparing a second edition that should make his outstanding Systematic Theology even better. See also Grudem's *"Free Grace" Theology: 5 Ways It Diminishes the Gospel* (Wheaton, IL: Crossway, 2016). Grudem's theology is sound, and his tone is just right.

9. Hoekema, Anthony A. *Saved by Grace*. Grand Rapids: Eerdmans, 1989. See chap. 12: "Sanctification" (pp. 192–233; see also 19–27, 47–67, 234–56). This revises and expands Hoekema's "The Reformed Perspective," in *Five Views on Sanctification*, ed. Stanley N. Gundry, Counterpoints (Grand Rapids: Zondervan, 1987), 61–90.

10. Keller, Timothy. Books, articles, sermons, interviews, etc. Keller masterfully applies the Bible. He penetratingly analyzes the culture and explains the views of his opponents in a disarming way. Here are six highlights: (1) *The Prodigal God: Recovering the Heart of the Christian Faith* (New York: Dutton, 2008). Both brothers in Jesus' famous parable rebelled, "but one did so by being very bad and the other by being extremely good" (p. 36). Elder-brother types "obey God to get things. They don't obey God to get God himself" (pp. 42–43). (2) *Counterfeit Gods: The Empty Promises of Money, Sex, and Power, and the Only Hope That Matters* (New York: Dutton, 2009)—what our idols are, how to discern them, and how to remove and replace them. Books 3–6 are probably the best all-around on those subjects: (3) *The Meaning of Marriage: Facing the Complexities of Commitment with the Wisdom of God* (New York: Dutton, 2011). (4) *Every Good Endeavor: Connecting Your Work to God's Work* (New York: Dutton, 2012). (5) *Walking with God through Pain and Suffering* (New York: Dutton, 2013). (6) *Prayer: Experiencing Awe and Intimacy with God* (New York: Dutton, 2014).

11. Mahaney, C. J. *Living the Cross-Centered Life: Keeping the Gospel the Main Thing*. Sisters, OR: Multnomah, 2006. Refreshing truths. You never graduate from the gospel—as if that is merely the ABCs of Christianity. It's the very heart of Christian living.

12. Murray, John. *Redemption: Accomplished and Applied*. Grand Rapids: Eerdmans, 1955. See especially chaps. 7–8: "Sanctification" and "Perseverance" (pp. 141–60). See also Murray's section on sanctification in his collected works: "Part V," in *Select Lectures in Systematic Theology*, vol. 2 of *Collected Writings of John Murray* (Carlisle, PA: Banner of Truth Trust, 1977), 277–317.

13. Naselli, Andrew David. *How to Understand and Apply the New Testament: Twelve Steps from Exegesis to Theology*. Phillipsburg, NJ: P&R

Publishing, 2017. Guides you to read and apply the New Testament carefully.

14. Naselli, Andrew David, and J. D. Crowley. *Conscience: What It Is, How to Train It, and Loving Those Who Differ*. Wheaton, IL: Crossway, 2016. Describes what conscience is, explains how to deal with your own conscience, and explains how to relate to other people when your consciences disagree.

15. Nichols, Stephen J., and Justin Taylor. Theologians on the Christian Life. Wheaton, IL: Crossway, 2012–present. This is a series—not a single book. This series is historically informed and warmly devotional. Some highlights: Fred G. Zaspel, *Warfield on the Christian Life: Living in Light of the Gospel* (2012); Michael Horton, *Calvin on the Christian Life: Glorifying and Enjoying God Forever* (2014); Dane C. Ortlund, *Edwards on the Christian Life: Alive to the Beauty of God* (2014); Matthew Barrett and Michael A. G. Haykin, *Owen on the Christian Life: Living for the Glory of God in Christ* (2015); John Bolt, *Bavinck on the Christian Life: Following Jesus in Faithful Service* (2015); Gerald Bray, *Augustine on the Christian Life: Transformed by the Power of God* (2015); Tony Reinke, *Newton on the Christian Life: To Live Is Christ* (2015); Sam Storms, *Packer on the Christian Life: Knowing God in Christ, Walking by the Spirit* (2015); Carl R. Trueman, *Luther on the Christian Life: Cross and Freedom* (2015); Joe Rigney, *Lewis on the Christian Life: Becoming Truly Human in the Presence of God* (2017).

16. Hughes, Barbara. *Disciplines of a Godly Woman*. Wheaton, IL: Crossway, 2001. (See next entry.)

17. Hughes, R. Kent. *Disciplines of a Godly Man*. 2nd ed. Wheaton, IL: Crossway, 2001. These two practical books by Kent and Barbara Hughes focus on your soul, character, ministry, and discipline.

18. MacArthur, John. *Faith Works: The Gospel according to the Apostles*. Dallas: Word, 1993. Soundly refutes Zane Hodges and Charles Ryrie by showing that you must repent to be saved and that good works and continuing to believe in Jesus are the necessary fruit of saving faith. (See the section "Charles C. Ryrie" in chap. 1 above.) See also two of MacArthur's other books on this issue: *The Gospel according to Jesus: What Is Authentic Faith?*, 3rd ed. (Grand Rapids:

Zondervan, 2008); and *The Gospel according to Paul: Embracing the Good News at the Heart of Paul's Teachings* (Nashville: Nelson, 2017).

19. Owen, John. *Overcoming Sin and Temptation*. Edited by Kelly M. Kapic and Justin Taylor. Wheaton, IL: Crossway, 2006. Responsibly updates the archaic language of Owen's classic works on how Christians mortify sin and how to understand temptation and indwelling sin. See also Matthew Barrett and Michael A. G. Haykin, *Owen on the Christian Life: Living for the Glory of God in Christ*, Theologians on the Christian Life (Wheaton, IL: Crossway, 2015).

20. Packer, J. I. *Keep in Step with the Spirit: Finding Fullness in Our Walk with God*. 2nd ed. Grand Rapids: Baker Books, 2005. Refutes higher life theology and presents a more excellent way. See also Packer's *Rediscovering Holiness: Know the Fullness of Life with God*, 2nd ed. (Ventura, CA: Regal, 2009); and *A Quest for Godliness: The Puritan Vision of the Christian Life* (Wheaton, IL: Crossway, 1990); as well as Sam Storms, *Packer on the Christian Life: Knowing God in Christ, Walking by the Spirit*, Theologians on the Christian Life (Wheaton, IL: Crossway, 2015).

21. Peterson, David. *Possessed by God: A New Testament Theology of Sanctification and Holiness*. New Studies in Biblical Theology 1. Downers Grove, IL: InterVarsity Press, 1995. Convincingly argues that the holiness word-group in the New Testament emphasizes definitive sanctification (which occurs at conversion), not progressive sanctification (which occurs throughout a Christian's life).

22. Piper, John. Books, articles, sermons, interviews, etc. Most are available for free at www.desiringGod.org. I suggest starting with Piper's signature book: *Desiring God: Meditations of a Christian Hedonist*, pages 11–359 in vol. 2 of *The Collected Works of John Piper*, ed. David Mathis and Justin Taylor (Wheaton, IL: Crossway, 2017): You most glorify God when he most satisfies you. Then *Future Grace: The Purifying Power of the Promises of God* (pages 13–419 in vol. 4 of *The Collected Works of John Piper*), which strategizes how to fight specific sins. Then *When I Don't Desire God: How to Fight for Joy* (pages 15–250 in vol. 6 of *The Collected Works of John Piper*), which follows up on *Desiring God*. Then *The Pleasures of God: Meditations on God's Delight in Being God* (pages 361–605 in vol. 2 of *The Collected*

Works of John Piper): God will most satisfy you when you know why God himself most satisfies God.

23. Piper, John, and David Mathis, eds. *Acting the Miracle: God's Work and Ours in the Mystery of Sanctification.* Wheaton, IL: Crossway, 2013. Theologically informed and pastorally wise. Shrewdly shows how to approach Christian living without being reductionistic. See especially the chapters by Piper (pp. 29–41, 127–38) and DeYoung (pp. 43–64).

24. Powlison, David. *How Does Sanctification Work?* Wheaton, IL: Crossway, 2017. The Yoda of biblical counseling explains how progressive sanctification works.

25. Sproul, R. C. *Pleasing God: Discovering the Meaning and Importance of Sanctification.* 2nd ed. Colorado Springs, CO: Cook, 2012. Clear introduction to Christian living by a master teacher.

26. Vincent, Milton. *A Gospel Primer for Christians: Learning to See the Glories of God's Love.* Bemidji, MN: Focus, 2008. Convicting four-part devotional: Part 1 presents thirty-one reasons you should regularly rehearse the gospel to yourself. Parts 2–3 are stirring prose and poetic versions of the gospel. In part 4, Vincent tells "the story behind the primer."

27. Warfield, Benjamin B. *Perfectionism.* Vols. 7–8 of *The Works of Benjamin B. Warfield.* 10 vols. New York: Oxford University Press, 1932. Probably the most technical resource in this list. Warfield pulls no punches when he analyzes higher life theology. See also works by Fred G. Zaspel, the leading expert on Warfield: *The Theology of B. B. Warfield: A Systematic Summary* (Wheaton, IL: Crossway, 2010), especially the section "Perfectionism and the Doctrine of Sanctification" (pp. 456–505); *Warfield on the Christian Life: Living in Light of the Gospel,* Theologians on the Christian Life (Wheaton, IL: Crossway, 2012).

28. Whitney, Donald S. *Spiritual Disciplines for the Christian Life.* 2nd ed. Colorado Springs, CO: NavPress, 2014. Gives strategies for growing as a Christian through Bible intake, prayer, worship, evangelism, serving, stewardship, fasting, silence and solitude, journaling, and learning. See also Whitney's *Praying the Bible* (Wheaton, IL: Crossway, 2015).

Acknowledgments

I'm grateful for friends who insightfully commented on the more detailed and academic version of this book: *Let Go and Let God? A Survey and Analysis of Keswick Theology* (Bellingham, WA: Lexham Press, 2010). Many thanks to friends who gave me feedback on this more popular-level book, especially Abigail Dodds, Tom Dodds, Andrew Johnson, Charles Naselli, Nate Weller, Jonathon Woodyard, and my teaching assistant, Matt Klem, who also prepared the indexes.

I'm grateful to my church's school, Bethlehem College & Seminary, for encouraging and empowering me to research and write in order to spread a passion for the supremacy of God in all things for the joy of all peoples through Jesus Christ.

Most significantly, my excellent wife, Jenni, has been supportive, interested, and sacrificial as I have researched higher life theology. This book's dedication page makes me smile every time I think about it: "To Jenni, my second blessing."

Subject and Name Index

Columbia Bible School, 18

Combs, William, 93

conscience, 81, 109

conversion, 11, 12, 16, 19, 20, 21,
22, 24, 33, 34n5, 35, 38, 42, 50,
58, 60, 62n17, 74n38, 77n1, 94,
104, 110

crisis, 9n5, 10, 11, 12, 13, 14, 15, 16,
17, 18, 19, 20, 21, 23, 24, 29, 32,
33, 35, 36, 37, 39–41, 42, 44, 46,
51, 66, 86, 88, 95

Crowley, J. D., 109

Cumming, J. Elder, 14–15, 91

D

Dallas Theological Seminary, 18,
21–27, 21n18, 23n24, 102

DeYoung, Kevin, 107, 111

discipleship, 27
disciple, 32, 42, 67, 69, 72, 72n,
73, 73n34, 75

E

evangelicalism, 18, 19, 19n, 21, 27

evangelicals, 7, 7n1, 9n5, 46, 103

F

fasting, 111

Ferguson, Sinclair, 3n5, 93, 107

filling with the Spirit, 2, 10, 18,
19, 20, 21, 22, 23, 24, 25, 29, 32,
35, 41–44, 43n30, 44nn33–35,
49, 62–69, 63nn20–21, 65n27,
66nn28–29, 74–75, 76n39, 88,
91, 107

Finney, Charles, 8, 11, 11n6, 12, 20

flesh, the, 23, 32, 39, 46, 55, 56, 57,
58, 59, 60, 68, 79–80, 80n10, 82,
83, 102

Fletcher, John, 8, 10, 20

Fox, Charles A., 16

free will, 11, 38, 38n13, 41, 48,
84–86, 99

G

glorification, 35, 50, 60, 78

Gordon, A. J., 19, 20

Gospel Coalition, The, 106

Gray, James M., 19–20

Griffith Thomas, W. H., 17–18,
22, 46

Grudem, Wayne, 25n29, 27, 93, 107

H

Harding, Mike, 93

Harford-Battersby, T. D., 13–14,
15, 87

Havergal, Frances Ridley, 17, 81

Haykin, Michael A. G., 109, 110

higher life movement, 8, 11–13,
18, 20

Hodges, Zane, 26–27, 109

Hoekema, Anthony A., 108

holiness movement, 8, 10–11,
20–21, 48n

Hopkins, Evan, 13–14, 15, 91

Horton, Michael, 109

Hughes, Barbara, 109

Hughes, Kent, 109

J

justification, 11, 12, 32, 37, 46, 49,
50–55, 52n5, 53nn8–9, 88, 104

Index of Scripture

2 Thessalonians

2:13 .... 51n3

1 Timothy

1:15 81

4:7–10 .... 82n21

6:11–12 .... 82n21

6:12.................... 67, 83

2 Timothy

1:7..................... 63n20

Hebrews

3:12–15 68

3:14........................ 89

12:1–3............... 82n21

12:14 68

12:14–16 .... 82n21

13:10 10

James

2:14–26 74

1 Peter

1:13–25 .... 82n21

1:15 67

1:22........................ 67

2:11 ....80, 82

2:11–18 .... 82n21

2 Peter

1:5–7 .... 82n21

3:14–18.............. 82n21

1 John

2:15................... 67, 68

2:15–16..............79–80

2:19.........................74

3:24 76

4:6......................... 89

4:15........................ 89

5:1........................... 89

Jude

19 58

21 68

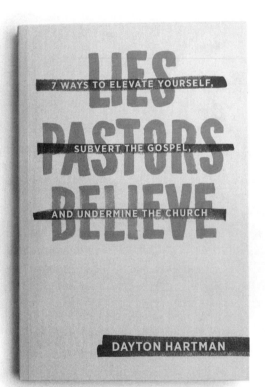

LEXHAM PRESS

A NEW VERSE-BY-VERSE COMMENTARY FOR PREACHING AND TEACHING

The Osborne New Testament Commentaries, by respected professor and author Grant R. Osborne, are for people seeking a straightforward explanation of the New Testament in its context, avoiding either oversimplification or technical complexity. Osborne brings out the riches of the New Testament, making each book accessible for all who consider themselves students of Scripture.

The Osborne New Testament Commentaries interpret Scripture verse by verse, bridging the gap between scholarship and the Church.

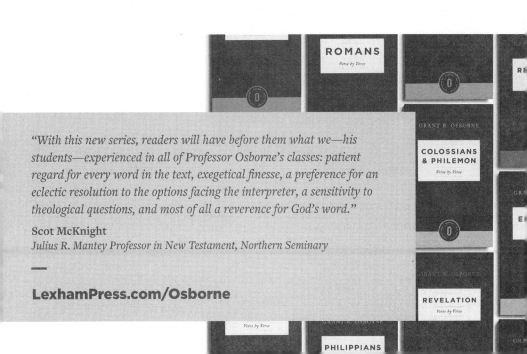

"With this new series, readers will have before them what we—his students—experienced in all of Professor Osborne's classes: patient regard for every word in the text, exegetical finesse, a preference for an eclectic resolution to the options facing the interpreter, a sensitivity to theological questions, and most of all a reverence for God's word."

Scot McKnight
Julius R. Mantey Professor in New Testament, Northern Seminary

LexhamPress.com/Osborne